**THIS BOOK IS DEDICATED TO THE WEATHER UNDERGROUND**

# WE ARE EVERYWHERE.
## WRITTEN IN COOK COUNTY JAIL.
## BY JERRY RUBIN

**HARPER & ROW, PUBLISHERS**
**New York · Evanston · San Francisco · London**

FIRST EDITION

STANDARD BOOK NUMBER: 06-013724-x

LIBRARY OF CONGRESS CATALOG CARD NUMBER: 77-154054

After *Do It!* I vowed never to write another book. Writing just takes too much out of me. The creative expression is fun, but the editing and re-editing is a drag. And even though *Do It!* was more than a book—it became a political event and myth—I don't see myself as a writer or "author."

But in the summer of 1970 I found myself locked up for 60 days in Chicago's Cook County Jail, that medieval dungeon. For the first week I was depressed, thinking of the friends, rock festivals and July 4th smoke-in that I was missing. A friend in jail, high up in the Mafia, kept suggesting to me that I write a book "about this hellhole." I decided to try, and I found that I ended my jail depression by pouring out my soul on paper every day.

I was in jail on a bullshit beef anyway. *It's tough being in jail: it's even tougher if you feel you're getting a raw deal.* I had just been through a five-and-a-half month federal conspiracy trial, been sentenced to five years for inciting to riot and two years contempt of court, and now the state of Illinois was threatening to put me on trial again for the same charges.

Illinois was pushing for a trial and I was worried about being found guilty and getting five years in Joliet, the state pen.

So a "deal" was worked out.

And the manner of the deal shows just how crooked is Amerikan injustice. The judge said he felt I had already been tried by a federal court and as far as he was concerned, the state charges should be dropped. The prosecutor said he personally didn't care much, but his boss did. **"How will it look in the papers if we let 'Jerry Rubin' off easy?"** he asked the judge. He further added that if the judge let me off, the prosecutors would publicly attack him in the press.

This conversation took place out of court and at a closed-door meeting between the judge, prosecutors and my lawyers. *(I had the room tapped.)* They were negotiating my freedom. It was decided to give me just enough time to satisfy the appetite of the prosecutors and keep the press happy— "just enough time so it won't look in the press like we're letting Jerry Rubin off."

I was offered 60 days, the first 30 to be served concurrently with a sentence in Virginia growing out of the 1967 Pentagon demonstration. I felt shitty about it, but I accepted 'cause 60 days is better than five years. So I pleaded guilty and resigned myself to a summer behind bars, happy knowing that I had hurt and would continue to hurt the USA government more than they could ever hurt me.

**Most of this book, then, is a journal that I wrote in longhand on loose-leaf notebook paper every day in Cook County Jail.** I'd wake up every morning at 4:30 A.M. along with the prisoners getting up for court call. I'd drink a cup of coffee and work myself into a writing stupor.

It was hard writing without grass, but I discovered that the stark barrenness of the jail environment produced a different kind of creative high. And often we also got grass and other psychedelics smuggled in.

I had to work early because later in the day the noise on the tier was so loud I couldn't hear myself think. I worked while everyone else was sleeping, hoping the guy two cells down would stop snoring and the guy five cells down would turn down his radio.

For seven hours until noon I just poured out my insides until my fingers hurt like hell, my mind felt like a block of wood, my body was exhausted and I was ready to spend the rest of the day and night rapping, getting strength from the example of the other prisoners and just walking the tier.

I was scared to death that a guard might rip off my notebook so I hid it under my mattress when I wasn't in the cell. I took it with me to meals and walks in the yard and I lied to the guards as to what I was doing.

Guards told me that if I was writing a book it would be taken away from me and burned when I was being discharged from the jail. *"You might be writing about how to escape from the jail and if it's published, guards could be killed and you'd be responsible. We couldn't let you take any written material out of here."*

So every week my lawyer came to see me and I tore out the pages I had written, hid them inside legal briefs and papers and held my breath as I was searched by guards on my way to a lawyer's conference. **Whew! Made it!** Then I'd exchange my legal papers with the journal inside, for other similar legal papers.

That's how I smuggled the book out of Cook County Jail.

When I got out of jail I had 120 pages of scrawled handwriting, about 100,000 words, spontaneous, stream-of-consciousness. I didn't censor myself. If I thought it, I wrote it down. The writing was all over the place, right out of my gut.

It concerned hundreds of subjects, including three recent jail experiences: I began to serve 30 days in Santa Rita Rehabilitation Center near Berkeley before the Conspiracy Trial started, then was moved across the country by federal marshals who wore miniature handcuffs as tie clasps, finished the 30 days in Cook County.

After the Conspiracy Trial I was in CCJ for two weeks until we got appeal bond. Then the summer 60-day sentence in Alexandria County Jail, Petersburg Reformatory in Virginia and Cooked County Jail.

After I got the writing all typed, I read it and dug it. But I felt it needed a lot of editing. I edited and re-edited and re-re-edited and re-re-re-edited.

Like everyone else I am going through a 1000 personal and political changes these days, and it was hard getting my ideas in final form. I read the book in its edited form and didn't like it. I put it aside, decided to kill the book, forget the whole fucking thing.

Finally, encouraged by friends, I went back to my original spontaneous journal and decided that it was better than all my editing. I learned a big lesson: **trust your spontaneity**.

Stew Albert worked for a week editing out repetitions and this book is that original journal, in its rough form, virtually as written every day in a Cook County cell. Parts have been added to bring the book up to date with my current ideas and some minimal editing has been done.

This book has become a collective project by people who like each other. Nguyen Ai Quoc Intercommunal Shitworkers Local 110 has done the layout. Almost all the photographs inside are by movement photographers from all over the country, and Nguyen Ai Quoc Intercommunal Shitworkers Local 110 went through 4,000 pictures to choose those which best reflect who we are.

Hundreds of people have contributed to the book in one way or another. I want to thank Stew, Beverlie Kane, Bill Schaap, David Fenton, Fran McCullough, Alan Katzman, Tom Miller, Judy Gumbo, Linda Evans, Bonnie, Jon, Paul, Maisie McAdoo, Tasha Simon, Doris Morgan, Sally Clark, Arthur Kinoy, Bobby Seale, Sharon Krebs, Lee Weiner, Nancy Kurshan. They are not responsible for all the nonsense in here, but they helped me get myself together, discussing style, politics and where all our heads are at.

We've tried to give as much of the work as possible to growing revolutionary collectives. For example, O.B.U. Typesetters, with the help of the Liberated Guardian, set the book in type. Soon we will publish and distribute books ourselves and won't need rip-off capitalist publishers.

**STEAL THIS BOOK!**


Writing is a poor substitute for person-to-person communication. I wish I could meet each of you personally. In *Do It!* I asked for letters and I received, and still receive, thousands of letters.

Beautiful letters. Incredible letters. I read each of them, but I find that if I try to answer them, I will be doing nothing else. The letters come from beautiful young people in high schools, colleges, freak communities, small towns, the army, Vietnam, suburban prisons, mental hospitals, jails. They reveal the breakdown of Amerika. Letters from young people of the ruling and working class.

These letters are so mind-blowing that Maisie McAdoo and Stew Albert have put them together in a book, titled *You*, which will be published shortly and which will blow you away.

I'd like to hear from you about *We Are Everywhere*. If you want to write me, write me care of my close friend and lawyer and I'll get it and try to answer it. My mail address is: Jerry Rubin, c/o Bill Schaap, 103 Park Avenue, New York, New York 10017.

**I especially want to thank undercover pig Bob Pierson and Warden Winston Moore of Cook County Jail for taking me away from my daily life with its business and hullabaloo and provoding me with free room and board so I could write this book.**

**The money the publishers will pay me for this book will be used to destroy Cook County Jail and every other jail and penitentiary in Amerika.**

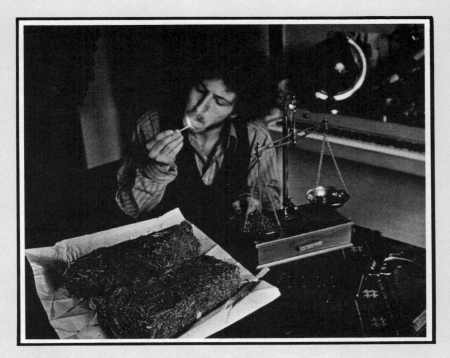

## STATEMENT TO MY ATTORNEY, RONALD J. CLARK

**Saturday, July 4**

One thing I learned in jail: You dream a lot! My mind becomes a series of Hollywood movies in technicolor and stereophonic sound with all my friends taking different roles.

You go to sleep wondering what world you will enter at night:

Love?

Violence?

War?

Dreams are great fun. Like going to a movie of your own unconscious. In jail your daily fantasies are reduced to walls and steel bars. At night you go to sleep and your unconscious is freed.

The reason jail is so bad is simple: the state is forcing you to plead guilty. Dig the procedure of going to court from Cook County Jail.

You are rudely awakened at 4:30 A.M. Your cell is clanged open and a guard orders you to get the fuck up. You get up and stand on your tier until 6—6:30 when you are marched down a hallway and packed into a small room

to wait there until 8 A.M. By 8 you have been up three and a half hours and then you are marched by number down a hallway and into another room where you wait until 10.

"Going to court is so shitty, man, you want to plead guilty just to get it over with!"

Packed like wild animals.

Ordered to move.

Strip.

*Spread your cheeks.*

In August, 1968, a guard stuck a rubber hose up your ass to see if you were hiding anything in there, a practice since outlawed.

The screaming and talking is so loud you can hardly keep your brains together. Then boom! You are pushed under armed guard into court, part of the savage machine of justice, a band around your wrist to remind you you're a prisoner, and you got to handle procedures you never understand, fast-talking lawyers, and a judge who has absolute power over your life.

You have died a full day already before going to court, and what you have to look forward to is standing in corridors and rooms a couple more hours before getting back to the freedom of your jail cell.

It must be hideous irony when getting back from court to your jail cell represents freedom!

For us as a generation the courtroom and jails may be becoming more important than the universities.

We are outlaws, enemies of the state. Our enemy owns the police, the courts, the jails. We are no freer than the poorest black woman or man in the darkest jail.

The purpose of jail is to force the prisoner to plead guilty to lighten the court load so judges can go home to the suburbs—and even worse, it is to break the weaker prisoners so they snitch on one another. Make a jail so bad that prisoners will do anything to get out, including testify against rap partners or allies. Be a stool pigeon in the Amerikan way, save yourself and send others to jail.

What happens when you arrest five for murder, all facing the electric chair

or life in prison, and then go to one and say: "Testify against the others and you will walk"?

Life in prison or freedom for a song!

*Sleep tonite at the Hilton or jail.*

We were sitting in the lock-up waiting for the marshals to chaperone us to court. Prisoners were exchanging their tales of despair. I said, "The 'G' can't get us to testify against each other 'cause we are a political movement." Ten eyes were on me as if I'd uttered a naïve silly statement. Hah! Hah!

"You know who turned this guy in? *His wife!*" "My rap partner turned me in!" "My brother!" Bobby Seale and I looked at each other.

"Do you have any unindicted co-defendants?" We had 18 but I *knew* none of them were going to testify for the enemy. "Is Stew Albert going to testify for the government?"

"If Stew testifies for the government, I think I'd quit the movement," said Bobby Seale, with that eyebrows-raised smile of his.

To those who see Panthers as racists, here was Seale saying he'd quit if blond, blue-eyed Stew Albert was a pig. Here was Bobby Seale, being framed to the electric chair. Offering his faith in revolutionary solidarity. Most of the prisoners are so burned by experience that they trust no one. NO ONE. And that is jailhouse wisdom—you must trust no one, not even your sister or brother. Living in a world of constant fear and mistrust can eat your heart out and cut off your life-giving oxygen. The world becomes dark. Our movement must never be overcome by the death of distrust. Jail takes life out of you by adapting you to a world of fearing everyone.

Bobby Seale had reason to fear and distrust. Yet by our statement and smiles we knew there was something special about the movement, something alive, real, beautiful, that made it the most: our sisters and brothers do not testify against each other to save their own individual skins.


Most dramatic moment in the trial comes when it's their turn to call their next witness. Our eyes are focused on the back room. Who will it be? Cabbage, the Justice Department lackey, goes back to get the witness. Will it be our best friend? We hope for some surprises, just to make the trial interesting. "C'mon Schultz, make it somebody interesting," I'd whisper to him.

The brown panel doors swung open.

Another cop. One copper after another, one FBI agent after another.

The FBI visited everyone barely connected with the Chicago convention demonstrations.

They went to people who had dropped out of active yippies and asked them to testify—went to parents, sisters, lovers, brothers—and came up with no one. They had no one from *our* side to testify for *them*.

The government's case was a B cops-and-demonstrators movie, but it was a better movie than our case. Accusing us of throwing rocks and bags of shit and marching down the street yelling "The streets belong to the people" is a better movie than saying we did not throw rocks or bags of shit.

The government was expressing our fantasies in their case.

I wish we had done what they said we did. Our myths were on trial.

*Each defendant had a myth which was on trial—and collectively we stood for the rebellion of young people.*

The trial became an international theatrical drama and its characters symbolic figures. The courtroom was full of caricatures, comic book characters. TV made the trial a worldwide soap opera, every night another chapter, kids versus parents, students versus teachers, prisoners versus the court system. Everyone had someone to identify with. It was impossible to be neutral.

Federal marshals in the courthouse used to quietly pull us aside and whisper into our ears, *"Will you autograph this so I can give it to my kid?"*

The lines of young people waiting to get into the circus began in the freezing cold at 3 A.M. outside the Federal Building. Kids waited seven hours to get in.

Taxi driver after taxi driver found out who we were and threw up the money changer saying, "This ride's on me. I'm with you guys. You're getting a raw deal. Some crazy judge you got, huh?"

People would often see us in restaurants and buy our meals for us and we got 1,001 invitations to dinners at homes.

We were the only people not searched as we came to court every day in the heavily guarded and armed Federal Building.

When we got to jail we were "The Chicago 7," like a bunch of foxy bank robbers who upstaged the pigs.

We were conquering heroes to the prisoners. "You guys did it!" We attacked the court system which had churned them up like meat in a sausage machine. We found so many prisoners who had been put behind bars by Hoffman or Schultz. Interracial humanhood, revolutionary black-white unity, is possible when middle-class whites join black people as enemies of the state, behind bars or as fugitives.

Maurie, the check forger, said to me the other day, "You really can't put in words what happens to a person's mind in jail." The mind flattens, deadens, you become a vegetable. You are oppressed not by brutality, but by boredom. Without stimulation your nerve ends wither.

The jails are breeding grounds for despair, action, hopelessness, criminals. A criminal is a potential revolutionary. Since revolution is illegal, a revolutionary is a criminal.

**We must see all crimes as political.** A country as rich as ours should not have one jail.

Every criminal is a political prisoner, a victim. Amerika, you created

Charlie Manson in your prisons. Can a country which murdered Indians, enslaved blacks, controls the world's resources, bombs Vietnam judge us? NO!

Can any white court judge the action of any black woman or man? We hide our guilt by saying blacks are violent when history shows black people to have been inexplicably patient and suffering and whites to have been the most violent race on earth.

As the cities fall under siege, the campuses blow up, guerrilla war rages throughout the world, the county prisons and penitentiaries of Amerika will explode one after the other.

The New York City jail riots only hinted at the anger of the sleeping dragons in Amerika's jails.

For any rebellion within a jail to win, people on the outside must take an active part. Revolts within a jail must be matched by demonstrations outside.

Prisoners live in a completely totalitarian state where the individual isn't worth shit. Only people on the outside can get the media to focus in on jail conditions. If people on the outside don't help, prisoners can be completely isolated and destroyed.

**Criminals, convicts and fugitives will lead the revolutionary armed struggle. The line between "crime" and "revolution" will wither away. Criminals will become revolutionaries, and revolutionaries will become criminals.**

Cook County Jail is an example of colonial rule: a largely black jail is run by black guards for the ruling whites. The warden and deputy warden are black. A black guard locks us up and says, "I'd rather be locking people up than be locked up." Amerika will try to solve its black problem by turning as many blacks as possible into prison guards.

Amerika will try to solve its "hippie problem" by turning as many hippies as possible into marshals at peace demonstrations, and after that, prison guards.

Most of the guards at Cook County Jail are like brothers off the block. If they didn't have jobs as guards, they might end up as inmates. Something happens to a person when he or she puts on a uniform.

He becomes his uniform.

He forgets the color of his skin, the history and soul of his people, and digs the authority.

What historical madness is at work when black GI's fight to kill Viet Cong? When black guards police black jails?

Millions of freaks the world over mourned and cried the day the assassin missed offing the Pope! What a pure yippie act of creative disruption! Weren't *you* sorry he missed?

## I DON'T TRUST ANYONE WHO DOESN'T GET STONED ALL OR MOST OF THE TIME.

We wanted to be indicted.

It was like getting a prime-time national TV show. The demonstration dealt a death blow to the Democratic Party. Yet if Humphrey had won, we would not have been indicted. The Democrats would not want to turn off the youth. Ramsey Clark was so outraged at the indictments that he testified for us—a real coup—which turned the ears of the prosecutors red.

The victory of the Republicans brought cowboy uptight Mitchell into office and he tried to preserve 1898.

*J. Edgar Hoover took over the White House.*

No more LBJ politics of consensus. We could hurt LBJ because we were part of his consensus. But to Nixon we do not exist.

For months we waited eagerly for the indictment. I prayed especially hard because I had already been indicted by a state grand jury for the same crime and if you can get a federal or state trial, prefer the federal.

A state trial would have raised few constitutional questions, generated little publicity, and had little symbolic meaning. I would have been up shit's creek. 10 years in the joint!

*What chance to win?*

Merely to arrest you is to put you up against the wall. The power to prosecute is fatal. What chance did I have to beat a Chicago jury? They'd send me to the pen for 10 years just so I'd get a haircut and shave. But in all analyses of government repression, we often do not take into consideration the human factor: I had a lazy prosecutor. I postponed the case eight to ten times, waiting for a federal indictment.

17

The grand jury was meeting and I ran up a $200 phone bill calling inside Washington reporters, Chicago crime reporters, trying to get a lead. Would there be indictments? I had the best yippie intelligence at work and we could find nothing.

*Then a tip!*

All would be indicted but me. I was crushed.

Nothing tasted good—not food; I couldn't even get high. I convinced myself the rumor was phony. Finally a newspaper blazed headlines: GRAND JURY TO INDICT 8. We were thrilled. We met and decided we'd call ourselves The Conspiracy.

The next day we were all destroyed by the report that since the Justice Department tapped our phones, a Supreme Court decision might force them to reveal one day Dave Dellinger called to find out the weather in Havana. Revealing the tapping of embassy phones might expose the USA for the voyeur it is.

Indictments were off.

We were the saddest motherfuckers around. I remember Rennie, Abbie, Dave and me meeting for supper and getting drunk (it was that bad. You get drunk when you want to forget something. You get stoned when you want to be real.) and commiserated, wondering what we were going to do now; now that we had failed to trick the government into indicting us. We wanted to use the trial as a national platform, to build a national organization, to expose repression.

## WE SOUGHT REPRESSION IN ORDER TO EXPOSE IT.

The dialectics of yippie revolution.

Some busts are good and some busts are bad. Got to force the government to indict you on your terms. Federal better than state. More publicity the better. Can't be yourself on trial—must be dissent, all young people. Going to jail is never good, except as a learning experience.

A week later I was home biting my nails wondering what to do with my state beef and all when I turned on the radio. "Eight indicted in Chicago!"

I had an Academy Award acceptance speech gathering dust in my drawer. I sent it out to the underground press, claiming Mitchell vetoed the indictments when he saw an advance copy of the statement.

I rushed to the phone, called up AP. "Who got indicted?" I stammered, words falling all over themselves. A voice gave the names: Rennie Davis, Abbie Hoffman, Jerry Rubin ... I screamed: "Yippie!" AP must have thought I was crazy. Then "Bobby Seale!" I fell on the floor. Bobby Seale!?

We must have a yippie running the Justice Department as well as the State Department!

*An alliance between the yippies and the Panthers!*

I rushed to call Abbie and all my friends. "Let's celebrate," I said to Abbie. In an hour the apartment was full with dope, champagne, cheering. Some straight New Left fellas came over to tell us how sorry they were. What fools!

*In a year we'd be household words.*

*In a year we'd incite more riots than our wildest fantasies.*

19

*In a year we'd expose and destroy the federal court system as unmercifully as we dusted off the Democratic convention. Yippie!*

Abbie and I knew that in our guts and that's why we're so happy, why the organization is called Yippie! Dave knew it too, and he'd admit it with a wink. Rennie would admit it intellectually, Tom Hayden would call us "crazy." Lee and John had a "How'd I get into this?" look.

Bobby Seale quoted Mao, "It is good if we are attacked by the enemy, since it proves that we have drawn a clear line of demarcation between the enemy and ourselves."

For weeks I walked 100 feet off the ground, then I locked myself in my apartment, with grass and rock music, and I wrote *Do It!* in two months.

I knew soon we'd be making history, and that's the greatest trip of all.

No one knew how, but we knew, that's all.


Next we needed good actors for the various roles. We needed a good judge. Preferably he should be a capitalist, a rich motherfucker, and since most judges are, we felt safe.

He should be as old as possible to dramatize the dinosaur quality of those who have power in Amerikan society.

We considered asking for a postponement of the trial for 25 years 'cause only the next generation can decide our guilt or innocence.

*A Hollywood production demanded a Hollywood typecast judge. Most of all, he should be a yippie.*

A yippie says everything that comes to her or his mind, all instinct.

The door opened, "Everybody Please Rise!" And there he was! It's Mr. Magoo! No, it's Elmer Fudd! "Oh, fuck," I thought, taking one look at this amazing creature, "he's too good, he's going to upstage us." Abbie was thinking the same thing.

Julius Hoffman—What? Hoffman? What Hoffman! Oh, too perfect, Abbie's illegitimate father! His face looked like it was chiseled out of stone. His voice was Scrooge-like, pure evil. His body had been frozen in ice and kept in cold storage since the last trial he presided over—the Spanish Inquisition. And then we heard the words we were to hear throughout the trial:

"I will not hear from you, sir. You have a lawyer to speak for you."

Abbie came to the arraignment in a Chicago copper's light blue shirt—he pleaded not guilty.

I liked Julie from the first moment I saw him. I hated and loved him. I loved his evil because it was so honest! Julie never hid his hate for us behind "judicial impartiality." He's a lovable fascist with a great sense of humor. He had the best lines in the trial.

We laughed through the whole trial—laughed at and with Julius. He proved to us that pigs can have a sense of humor.

## I DON'T TRUST ANYONE WHO'S NEVER DONE TIME

If I had not been indicted, I might have considered suicide. Psychological war could be much more effective than outright repression. I know the government does not have a psychiatrist advising them. Just knowing you are going to miss history was enough to send you on a massive bummer.

Collective living is our ideal. But here in Cook County life is an enforced, unhealthy collective. Amerika does all it can to destroy any feeling for collective life. Jail is like the army is like a mental hospital is like kindergarten is like school. You learn in jail to eat with a spoon out of a tin plate and cup, eating in the line. Why does food have to be such shit? Everyone has a sad story, and the most shocking thing is if you ask the backgrounds of the black and white prisoners, it is Vietnam!

*From Nixon's army to Nixon's penitentiary.*

Tonight a fight broke out in the day room over what TV program to watch and everyone was locked up in their cells. Then the lieutenant came and lectured us. "If a fight starts, fellows, break it up." ("Hah, I'm not going to get my head split open and another beef trying to break up a fight.") "Tell the officer." ("I'm no snitch.")

Today in court, one guy told his judge, "No, I'm not going back there. Anything but jail." Frightened, scared, he panicked and turned and ran and was gunned down by a cop in the courtroom, wounded and taken to the hospital. Court is a highly middle-class scene requiring technical skills, way above the education of most of the poor prisoners.

I'm in the new tier painted pink and white! The air is heavy inside a jail. Really, the air of jail and free air smells different.

Your world is so small, a six by eight cell. What happens to you when your world is reduced to six by eight feet? Day follows day in deadening monotony.

The little things make each day a new adventure: On Monday you change sheets, Tuesday is commissary, Wednesday, one and a half hours in the yard.

People in a fight are taken to the hole for 10 days, just the floor with a hole, no bed, no light, food once a day. I've heard people going crazy there, pounding on the walls with no one to listen.

*A totalitarian police state requires absolute control of information.* Long before Spiro leveled his rifle at the head of Walter Cronkite, we told the reporters at our daily trial press conferences that their heads were next to go.

The day is not far off when political commissars appointed by Spiro Agnew will censor the national TV news and newspapers and magazines, and completely outlaw the underground press.

In fact what was the first move the judges made before the trial began?

Bar the press.

Bar demonstrations inside 120 feet of the Federal Building.

Cook County Jail and federal marshals absolutely prohibited the press from any contact with Bobby Seale, so that Bobby's version and vision could never be expressed to the public except through notes smuggled out or through our voices. By already being a prisoner, Bobby was naturally goaded to the desperation that resulted in his rising politically and demanding his rights in the courtroom.

It was the press which decisively settled the Battle of August, 1968. Images of police viciousness and brutality—everyday life in Amerika—flashed across the TV screens. Cronkite even called it a "police state" and the Democrats were washed with blood.

**From that week on, policemen became pigs.**

Student street fighting spread across the land. TV spread the riots by spreading the information, which is just another way of saying reality creates more reality.

Spiro is only pissed off that the right cannot manipulate the media as well as we can. With the hardhat marches, they are catching on. But it is not a technical skill, or a conspiratorial one, it is history which decides who can best use the media. We used to hold daily press conferences until they got too

repetitive to dramatize and explain what was really going on. The courtroom is no place to discover truth. Everything important is "irrelevant and immaterial."

The jury never found out that Ramsey Clark was kicked off the witness stand until the trial was over and they read it in the papers. The prosecution had the judge on their side; we had the press on ours.

**REPRESSION MUST BE SECRET.**

It is only fear of exposure which prevents the pigs from really spilling the blood of blacks and freaks.

Two months after the trial the Honorable Julius was invited to the White House as a conquering inquisitor—another one of Nixon's Patton-like heroes, along with Clement Haynsworth, defeated Supreme Court judge—and when Julius and Pat Nixon met who did they condemn? The media.

For us there is nothing the press can say that makes us look bad. The worse they portray us, the greater heroes we are to youth.

In fact we preferred right-wing coverage to the liberals: the right saw the trial as a super-sport event, magnified our evil to yippie levels, and helped every observer participate in the event.

*New York Times* coverage was an endless search for the "issues" of the trial, an attempt to translate courtroom drama into rational interchange.

Tony Lukas often wore the saddest face in the courtroom as he watched The Battle and knew he could never report it. All life was penciled out of his stories, vivid description cut into the dead frame of the *New York Times* obituary page. There is more truth in one New York *Daily News* headline than in 500,000 columns of *New York Times* crap.

The *Times* takes the blood and emotion out of events.

Lukas flew to New York for an emergency crisis meeting, then flew back. But he was a defeated man. To what extent was censorship in New York entering his own bloodstream and forcing him to censor himself before he ever got to the typewriter? **Self-censorship is more vicious than overt direct censorship.**

You know what your boss wants and you fit yourself to suit his needs to avoid a direct ugly clash in which he has all the power. When Julius "shouted," the *New York Times* blue penciled Lukas's verb to "said." The word was clear: No description of the judge.

The media got on Julius's nerves by revealing that while young kids stood in line all through the night in biting, freezing cold, many of them having driven two hundred miles to get there, then being watched during the trial for any show of support by hawklike marshals and ejected, members of Chicago High Society sat in the press and other front-row seats calmly and innocently explaining, *"Why, Julie let us in."*

That infuriated Julie.

What right did the press have to print such garbage? After all it is MY courtroom.

The *Times* will print the putting of one million black and hippie people into concentration camps in cold, black and white formal language, using the euphemistic language of the government ("Vietnamization" means put the gooks on the front lines and let them get blown up by mine bombs, etc.), with a long news analysis right next to the column. You'd never know it was real human beings, your sisters and brothers, being carted away like animals.

The *Times* is able to destroy your sensory perception of injustice and turn potential anger into intellectual nothingness.

We were being railroaded in the courtroom—our only hope was mass popular reaction.

If the press covered every trial the way they covered us, the chances of combatting courtroom terror would be increased. But the press is not interested in the steady march of black people from the ghetto to jail to court to jail. In that courtroom we were fighting for everybody screwed by the judicial nightmare. If the Chicago 8 trial was like that, wow! Imagine what goes on daily in every courtroom in this country.

When an innocent black woman or man is railroaded into jail for one to ten years, that is not news.

We tried to use our TV trial to spotlight the injustice in all the courtrooms. Before our trial, even young people thought some sort of fair justice took place in the courts. They accepted it on faith. No more!

## Sunday, July 5

A battle in a courtroom is between unfair opponents. The prosecution has an incredible advantage. The prosecution had large offices in the Federal Building, whereas we had to do our legal work in restaurants and over-crowded apartments.

The "G" had unlimited funds whereas we had to beg, borrow and rip off.

The prosecutor and judge go out the same door, go to the same restaurants, work for the same boss. They tap our phones, we don't tap theirs. They intimidate, frighten our witnesses—our first was fired the day after he testified. If we tried to intimidate theirs, we'd be off to their jail for centuries.

With Bobby in jail we had to hold our strategy meetings in a jury room made available by marshals. We assumed the room was bugged. That assumption fucked our heads up. We always assumed they knew our strategy the next day.

The prosecution table always is right next to the jury while our table is across the room. When the prosecutor says, "Good morning, Jury," that's human kindness; when we say it, it's trying to influence the jury and contempt of court. Jurors became employees of the government and they felt some loyalty to their benefactor.

We got very excited when we snuck a wino on the jury.

He came to the jury box stoop-shouldered, dirty, unbuttoned white shirt, sloppy pants. He'd know the enemy!

After one week on the jury, he underwent a personal transformation: new horn-rimmed glasses, black suit, erect posture. He moved from rummy-dump fleabag hotel to a fancy suite in the Palmer House. One look at him and we knew he was going to repay his struck-it-rich supporters with a guilty vote.

Later we found he was one of the hang-'em hardliners.

Federal marshals took care of the jurors, chaperoned them, fed them, answered their every need and whim, entertained them.

Hip to what was going down, we made a motion that we pay half their salary and yippie marshals take care of the jurors half the time.

*Yippie marshals!*

Everyone in the courtroom saw it as a put-on yippie motion. It was the most serious move we made through the whole trial. I'm sure the incestuous relationship between marshals and jurors turned them against us. All it takes is a nod in the right place, a shake of the head. The jurors know what is expected of them.

You know what we found out long after the trial ended? Ron Dumbrowski, the judge's private marshal, who responded to the judge's orders by going over to us and staring two cold death eyes and shouting, "Be quiet, Mr. Dellinger!"—the same marshal who we'd laughed and cursed at—"Would you shoot us if the judge told you to, Nazi Ron?"—was the jurors' private chaperone.

He lived with them and cared for them.

**Our chief policeman was their closest friend!** Naturally their sympathy would be with him as we fought him.

What a farce is a jury trial! They accuse us of making the trial a farce. Hah! The trial was a farce. We exposed it, we forced the system to reveal its soul—and there wasn't much soul there—only an evil crooked deck of cards.

The trial went from one crisis, turning point, high spot to another.

Every day a new trial, another adventure!

Every day better and more exciting than the previous one. I awoke every morning excited to life to go to court.

Suspense, drama, surprise!

Never a dull moment!

Even the dull moments were exciting when you meditated on what was going down. Dig the environment. It was a total environment, what Jeff Shero called a time machine. You had the feeling nothing was going on anywhere else in the world. I used to get stoned and just sit in the courtroom staring at faces and laughing. Everyone so well typecast for their role. And let anyone start taking the escapade serious, there were the artists with their huge pads moving from row to row to get a good shot and then drawing your picture.

Now how can you believe the show when five feet away three artists are busy drawing you for the evening news! CBS artist Howard Brody would sit on the edge of his seat, eyes bulging out, mouth dripping with the saliva of excitement, adrenalin glands a'running, 350 different colored pencils falling all over his lap, and constantly staring at you for his drawings.

*You didn't want to turn your back or your head away 'cause you didn't want to make things rough for ol' Howard.*

Look a little my way, Jerry, Howard would unconsciously say to you. Howard turned us all into movie-TV actors. Howard didn't create the theater. The theater was already there.

After the trial we'd watch TV and see another trial, a different trial than the one we had attended all day in the courtroom. There was Kunstler, arms flailing to the skies, feet flying. Now I never once saw Bill in that pose.

But CBS always put an extra flourish in the arms.

**Makes a better drawing, you know. Since color TV is where it's at, I used to wear bright colors every day to court: red pants, green pants, yellow polo shirt with red lines, multicolored headband, incredible tie-dye shirts.**

Bobby Seale suggested once that all of us wear all black one day to court.

One of the reasons we temporarily gave up on the trial movie we were planning is we knew we could never find an actor who could capture Julius. We offered Julie $100,000 to play himself, but he never even answered our letters. We then offered the part to Groucho Marx but he refused, too. Dustin Hoffman came to the trial for a week to study Julius to maybe play him in a future melodrama—so we shall see. Right on, Ratso!

The sketches made the vicious prosecutor, Schultz, look so cherubic, earnest and baby-faced. Like a soft college intellectual.

Actors become known by their sketchability. Abbie's wild hair, gigantic nose, enormous teeth made him a ball to sketch.

Dellinger and Kunstler were tough motherfuckers to catch with a pen.

My beard and long hair made me easy but I was always sneering.

Lee came up looking like Karl Marx. Lennie Weinglass like a matinee idol. Rennie came out as the boy next door. Sketches tried to bring out our essence, but in reality reduced our personality to an image.

We became cartoon characters.

And then in addition to the World, there was another invisible personage in the room, a spirit, affecting everyone's behavior: History. We knew generations from now would read about our trial. It was in the tradition of Socrates, Jesus, Willie Sutton, Galileo, Scopes, Sacco and Vanzetti, the Rosenbergs. Part of us wanted to lose so we would make a bigger impact on history.

*"Can you think of any trial throughout history in which the defendants won?"* asked Abbie. The winners are forgotten in the dustbin of history. Socrates lost; Jesus lost; Sacco and Vanzetti lost.

That gave us something to think about.

Before the trial started we worried about being assassinated or assaulted in the streets of Chicago. Abbie suggested we ask for a bullet-proof courtroom. It was perverse as we soon discovered: we were the home team. We were the underdog. We thought we wouldn't be able to walk the streets except with bodyguards. It was the other way around!

Julius Hoffman couldn't walk the streets except surrounded by a phalanx of marshals. He once went to visit his sick wife in the hospital and was literally chased out of the place by furious doctors and orderlies and nurses. Julius's phone was unlisted but our spies got it and somehow Julius started getting funny phone calls—he had to change his number 12 times.

Julius lived in fear, marshals permanently stationed outside his luxurious apartment.

He didn't even want to go to parties any more because someone was always asking him that question with critical eyes.

We were overwhelmed with requests to appear everywhere. Every week every defendant and lawyer flew to every end of the USA to speak before overflowing crowds of college students where Julius Hoffman's name was automatically followed with boos and heckling laughter, and we were treated like Amerika in the forties treated its World War II veterans.

*We discovered a new problem for a revolutionary to deal with: autograph seekers.* Is it counterrevolutionary to sign an autograph? But isn't it counterrevolutionary to refuse to sign a fifteen-year-old kid's request for our autograph?

Money poured in from all over the country: our fight was the fight of the people. We had more speaking requests than we could fulfill. It became news what we did and thought.

Abbie's name began popping up in the gossip columns.

Movie producers and directors, playwrights, newsmen, authors, talent scouts all fought each other to have lunch with the defendants.

*We didn't know whether we were going to jail—or Hollywood.*

Mail flowed into the Federal Building. Abbie got one letter addressed simply to: Abbie Hoffman, Chicago, Illinois. Julius Hoffman became our private mailman.

Young people started writing us telling us their personal problems. Every morning and afternoon in court began with the huge delivery of mail and we began the trial day reading our mail.

When I began the trial I had a vision, a dream. This intense experience would transform seven individuals into One, a family. To participate in a war, a long battle, is exciting if it is a *shared* experience. To do that each of us would have to throw ourselves into the collective. Few better opportunities have been given to create a revolutionary group than our trial. But that would demand that we all live together.

Separate living in Amerika through apartments—with separate bank accounts—perpetuates the loneliness and separation that drives most Amerikans batty.

We couldn't get our shit together. Previous antagonisms from organizing the crime in the first place could not be overcome, between Abbie and me on

We think transportation should be FRIENDLY and FREE and go where people need to go. Private cars isolate people and foul the environment.

imagine a city on FREE WHEELS

one side, and Rennie and Tom on the other. Hayden was the only one of the five of us really pissed off at the indictment. It took him away from organizing in Berkeley.

From the moment of the indictments Tom's position was consistent, however reprehensible I found it: Most important thing is to win the case with the jury. Sitting in the courtroom we are on their turf, and we should do nothing which might get us contempt 'cause that would mean jail (too extreme) for no reason at all. Our survival is the most important thing. And most of all, let's get the trial over with as soon as possible and get back to real revolutionary work. You can't do anything in their courtroom. If all fails, we must be sure not to alienate, through courtroom antics, the liberals of the Appellate Court because the appeal bond is the most important issue.

We should organize the good liberals against repression.

*What a drag.*

Hayden's position was that we should not work as a collective. Instead, if one defendant opposed something, we shouldn't do it. Hayden's facial expressions killed many an idea and turned our meetings from turn-on sessions which they should have been to bickering, useless personality conflicts, wrangling.

Tom felt the Conspiracy Trial was not that important an event, and that we should not try to build it into either a national myth or organization. This was all weird, because Tom made these arguments from a left-wing point of view. He said armed self-defense was the main task for revolutionaries today. Since armed struggle was suicidal in the courtroom, Tom argued, we should concentrate on winning over the jury through rational arguments and good behavior.

35

Tom's position brought him into direct conflict with Dave Dellinger, whose moral politics lead him to fight tyranny wherever he is, and Abbie and me, who saw the trial as an opportunity to inspire a children's crusade.

The yippies felt the most important goal of The Conspiracy should be the destruction of the myth of the Amerikan judicial process. We tried to balance that with winning over the jury too—if it was possible. But we were on trial to have a good time, and to use the media and guerrilla theater, humor, fun and rage to expose Amerikan injustice to young people.

Tom's attitude during the trial is important because it is a symptom of a

general movement hang-up—using revolutionary rhetoric as an excuse to sit on your ass.

**Beware the revolutionary who gives left-wing reasons for doing nothing.**

Too many revolutionaries these days say they can't bother themselves any more with rallies, demonstrations or guerrilla theater because, "I've got a piece and I'm going to kill a pig."

Revolution becomes (talking about) offing pigs and nothing else.

Instead of the armchair academic revolutionary, we have the armchair pig-killer.

Yippies believe in using *real* guns or *toy* guns depending on the vibes of the situation.

Tom's position was strengthened because John Froines, indicted by surprise, also felt avoiding contempt or a guilty verdict were the most important

things: Hayden and Froines formed the conservative do-nothing wing of the Conspiracy Trial.

Such political differences made it impossible for us to live together. In fact we relished our time apart; we got sick of being with each other every day. Fuck, all of us never even got stoned together once!

And one of the reasons we didn't try harder to work it out by living communally was because we all had loving, monogamous relationships with wives or girlfriends that we thought satisfied our emotional needs.

The *male supremacy* of the Amerikan government prevented it from indicting any women who were active in destroying the Democratic convention. Therefore the defendants were all male, and women were forced into the role of emotional supporters and staff workers.

The men were on trial, and the women were behind them. Having huge competitive egos, and being at the center of the media storm, we defendants did not try to overcome this hypocrisy in our lifestyle.

Women were the unsung heroes of the trial. We got all the glory and electronic back-massaging but women did most of the nitty-gritty work. Women carried out the research, behind-the-scenes arrangements and office work that never rated a press conference.

And a lot of the hullabaloo caused in the courtroom was created by the women who were on their feet cussing out the judge every chance they got. I don't know how many times a punching and kicking Nancy, Gumbo, Ann, Anita, Susan, Donna, Sharon, Tasha, Michelle, etc., was carried out of the courtroom by the marshals.

The domination of the women by the men, plus the monogamy that bred exclusiveness and made each defendant a world unto himself, caring about ourselves first, made life outside the trial around The Conspiracy a whirlwind.

*Right out of Hollywood.*

The Conspiracy broke into political and social factions: pacifist Dave and the violent yippies on one side; Tom and John Froines on the other; Rennie Davis in the middle, closer to us politically but closer to Tom personally, and trying to tone down tempers and hold everything together as a mediator; Lee off on his own in his own world.

Tom lived with one of our lawyers, Lennie Weinglass, in an apartment that became the staff and Mob center; Dave lived with his family thirty miles outside the city and drove to the trial every day; Rennie lived with Susan Gregory; Lee with Sharon Avery; John with Ann Froines; Abbie and Anita Hoffman stayed in their own room with a Chicago family; Nancy Kurshan and I rented an apartment in Hyde Park.

Nancy and I even brought with us from New York to Chicago our one possession in the world, a color TV.

You could tell the political faction by where they ate. We were the live-it-up faction. Abbie, Anita, Dave, Bill, Nancy and I went to a restaurant every day at the lunch break and ate big meals. Kunstler and I shared a piece of cheesecake after meals.

We believed in enjoying ourselves while we could. Revolution does not mean puritanism. Revolution does not mean asceticism. Revolution does not mean deprivation or self-sacrifice and self-punishment.

We Commies should out-promise all the bourgeois politicians because we have more to offer—socialism will mean *more*, not less, for the people of the world.

Communism and revolution have for too long been identified with the propaganda of economic deprivation, soup lines and rice diets.

Once Stew Albert cut through a lot of left-wing white guilt by saying, "Socialism does not mean crowded living conditions."

*Food for all!*

*Everything for everybody!*

*Pot in every home!*

Technology makes it possible for every human being in the world to enjoy a fantastic surplus standard of living if we could rescue the machines away from the capitalist greedy.

*Every woman, every man an artist!*

And we'll enjoy ourselves, not suffer, while living and making the revolution.

We have to destroy a selfish capitalist system of rich and poor—but our Communism will be hedonistic!

The restaurant reserved a big table for us every day and we ate well while planning the afternoon's court strategy, rehearsing witnesses, laughing, giggling and breaking up over the day's hijinks.

*The trial became a way of life.*

Restaurants oppress waitresses and waiters by forcing them to serve other people. They humiliate waitresses by forcing them to beg for tips. Restaurants also divide the people into classes with varying privileges.

After the revolution bourgeois restaurants will not exist, and all the people will share and eat more organic and tasty foods. There will be no tipping, and we'll all take turns serving each other.

Jail must be the saddest place on earth.

Politics aside, I feel sympathy with everyone behind bars, airmen in North Vietnam, capitalist agents in Cuba, hash smugglers languishing in dungeons in Turkey, intellectuals and hippies in Russia.

We just finished visiting day in jail. It's the high point of the week—but also the low point 'cause when it's over you return to your cell and your visitor leaves.

Today two wives of prisoners fainted during the visit. One Puerto Rican woman was pregnant and she collapsed.

In jail to hope is to expose yourself, to make yourself vulnerable, to open yourself to sadness. I just rapped with Herman. He's been in jail three weeks now. Police stopped him on the South Side and found him with a gun. "I carry it for my own protection," he said, " 'cause everyone over fourteen has a gun, you got to protect yourself against all the gangs who are shooting each other."

He was booked and charged with possession of firearms, a misdemeanor, but when he got to court he was charged with armed robbery, accused of robbing a taxi driver two months earlier for $125! The cab driver didn't show up at court. Bail set up at $10,000, or $1,000 to walk, way beyond Herman's means. "I got a wife and two kids. I didn't do no armed robbery." The charge carried one to ten years in the penitentiary.

*Herman has no lawyer.*

The public defender, who works with the prosecutor and judges to "clear the calendar" and avoid costly trials, asked Herman to plead guilty and take a year. So he languishes in Cook County Jail, awaiting a trial. Sadness etched into his face. Lawyers, especially public defenders, do not care about these defendants. They are "case" numbers, statistics.

**You walk up and down the tier stir-crazy. You stare at the cell. You hate the jail and the judge but that's too bad—they're too powerful—so you hate yourself. You hate your fellow prisoners.**

I arrived at the tier where Jack, the head of the Mafia, was held after being sentenced to five years, along with his brother. When I arrived they immediately abandoned their card game, asked who I was, offered me oranges, cookies, toothpaste, envelopes, a cell next to them and wide arms and smiles. We—me, hairy Commie yippie dope addict, and he—fifty-six, bald, gambler, rich—recognized we were both political prisoners. They fixed up my room, tied up a clothesline and moved me closer to them.

*Jack bought $50 of commissary every week and gave it all out free to the prisoners.* He told me he accepted his five years, as he got it, "like a man."

"I was railroaded! They had a stool pigeon on the stand and you know, I never saw the sonovabitch before in my life.

"The jury came back after 12 hours and said they were hung on me.

"The judge ordered them back to reach a verdict. It was Saturday morning and they wanted to be home for the weekend, so in an hour they came back with a guilty verdict. Ain't that something? Well," he shrugged philosophically, "it's an occupational hazard. The government has had 100 feds on me for the past 10 years. The press has crucified me. If you can't stand the heat, get out of the kitchen."

*Jackie didn't mind my Communist ideas but he tried every way to get me to shave and he didn't like the fact that I didn't bathe as often as he did.* He showered three to five times a day. When he left to go to the joint I was depressed for a day. Maybe even Commie revolutionaries and Mafia capitalists can get together behind bars as criminals. We didn't agree on politics, but we shared hot chocolate, tea, coffee together, and exchanged jail stories.

The effect on the jailer is lousy. Power over others knocks out your humanity and turns you into a mad sadistic animal.

## Monday, July 6

Santa Rita County Jail has a strict policy: every inmate must get his hair cropped to one or one and a half inches within 24 hours of arrival at the institution.

It is their way of rehabilitating you through humiliation. One of the first things done in the concentration camps in Nazi Germany was to shave *all* the hair off inmates' heads and bodies.

I had not gotten a haircut in two years or a shave in one year and I felt sick at this destruction of my identity.

I felt very sick about it all.

The trial was due to begin in a month and I was going to be shaved, like an inmate of a concentration camp. My hairless appearance would be a testimony to the repression and sexual violence and jail oppression of Amerika—what a drag.

**IT IS MORE EXCITING TO BE A SYMBOL OF FREEDOM THAN A SYMBOL OF SUFFERING.**

Amerika asks us, "Why the beards, hairy legs, arms and long hair?", but we ask Amerika, "Why do you do the unnatural act of cutting your hair and shaving the beautiful hair off your face and body?"

Our hair prevents Amerika from seeing its reflection in our face—therefore we are a living rejection of its misdeeds and violence—our hair is our picket sign and our Molotov cocktail. Our hair hurts/offends them more than anything we can say or do.

*Hair naturally grows—to cut it or shave is unnatural.*

I had been denied my individuality, denied my humanity.

The state had decided for me how I should look.

I had finally discovered the person in me that I liked.

For the first 21 years of my life I'd shaved once a day—what a waste of time!—and got a haircut every three weeks.

When I took my first radical act, visiting Cuba in 1964 with 84 others in a

41

trip banned by the State Department, I decided to let the hair above my lip and under my nose grow. Soon I had a mustache—from a straight clean ex-newspaperman, sports reporter and college student, an anarchist activist was born.

The handlebar mustache transformed my identity.

From there it was a short step to dropping out of school and organizing anti-war demonstrations. But my hair was still short—and I used to wear white shirts and sports coats with holes in them.

The birth of the hippies in 1966 liberated me from protestor to revolutionary and enemy of the state as I let my hair grow long.

**The prison uniform for men in Amerika is the white shirt, tie and sports coat or suit.**

**The prison uniform for women is girdles, bras, stockings, high heels and a painted and perfumed mask.**

That uniform symbolizes the fact that you owe your soul to Business Amerika, the necktie around your neck is like a hangman's rope around your neck.

The uniform means you are working for Someone Else.

You must arrive at work at a certain hour and leave at a certain hour and you must look a certain way to fit the expectations of everyone else in the Amerikan prison.

Business Amerika is just an extension of the army and the jails.

The jails enforce their rule by forcing everyone to look alike. So do the schools. So business. Rebellion begins on your face. Long hair, beards, no bras and freaky clothes represent a break from Prison Amerika, a rejection of

the God is White Milk, cleanliness-is-godliness values and the birth of us as a new nation of freaky artists.

We are not alienated artists because our art is our way of life. The yippies were on trial in Chicago for combining lots of hair, dope, freaky clothes with disruptive demonstrations and international revolution.

Sadly, I was led into the barber's chair. An inmate, a black inmate, was forced to do the cutting. I slipped him a pack of cigarettes not to make it too short. But the head pig sat watching and he ordered the prisoner to keep cutting. Cut, cut, cut. Destroy, destroy, destroy.

**Amerika loves to destroy the culture of native minorities, from blacks to Vietnamese—and now we, Amerika's children, had become a foreign minority whose local cultures were being destroyed, raped by an imperialist culture. Cutting our hair is an act of cultural genocide.**

I'll never forget the expression on my co-defendants' faces when they met with me finally in the lock-up and saw my new appearance.

They gasped.

Abbie said, "Jesus, you look like the Free Speech Movement—like you did three years ago. It's awful!" Kunstler tried to make me feel better. "Hey, you're really handsome underneath all that hair." But I felt sick to my stomach. For the first three weeks of the trial I was ashamed to look in the mirror. I began to hate myself—which, of course, was the goal of the head and face rape in the first place.

Then Abbie and Lee came up with a brilliant idea, to turn my haircut into an act of theater: a wig! Yippies from all over Amerika would be asked to cut

a lock of their hair and mail it to me c/o the Federal Building so that I could turn the hair of all my sisters and brothers into a beautiful wig to wear the rest of the trial until my hair grew back.

Better than that, we'd have a contest!

Julie was stone bald and wow did he need hair. "Send a lock of your hair to your favorite yippie—Jerry or Julius. The one who gets the most hair wins a pound of dope."

At a sacred moment before court ceremony one morning Abbie and Lee sat in a barber's chair and symbolically cut one lock of their hair and at a ceremony at the beginning of court presented their locks of hair to me.

News of the yippie contest was published in the underground press and within days envelopes with hair from all over the country began flooding into me from every state in the union. Brown hair. Black. Red. Green. Yellow. Curly. Straight.

All hair was attached to a note explaining the religious significance of each yippie donating a part of herself or himself for myself.

*Tons of hair.*

Sometimes 30 letters a day.

I'd open the boxes, packages and letters and pour the hairs out on the defense table for the press, jury and Julie to see—a testimony to the loyalty and sisterhood and brotherhood and solidarity of yippies across Amerika.

Julie must have been receiving tons of hair too.

Wonder how he felt when locks of hair fell out of 10 straight envelopes! I got letters from communes and underground papers where members got together and had cut a lock of their hair and mailed it to me.

The notes said they were mailing some to Julie too 'cause they couldn't decide which yippie was more deserving.

Julie never acknowledged the receipt of hair but maybe that scowl on his face was because he'd just opened his mail?

I won the contest and one day I came to court with a long flowing bush-haired wig.

I put the wig on in the morning and took it off at night. I was a longhair again.

Suddenly spectators and press and marshals came up to me and said, *"Wow, your hair grew back fast."*

Sometimes I'd take a naïve liberal behind a corner and dramatically yank off the wig. The liberal would scream and faint.

Before the wig, Schultz and Foran used to ask witnesses, "Did Jerry Rubin look like that during the convention week?" "No," was the pig's answer, "his hair was much longer then." Once I wore the wig those comments stopped. I wanted to rip off the wig some time dramatically before the jury as a lark.

But I worried about alienating the jury.

The woman in the first row wore a red wig and I figured two or three other jurors might be wearing wigs.

Wouldn't they be offended?

I decided to wait till the right moment and if the right moment never came I wouldn't do it. The moment came unexpectedly one morning.

A Red Squad cop testified he saw me screaming, "Kill the pigs!" in the middle of a rock-throwing riot. It was an absolute lie.

"Did Jerry Rubin look as he does now?" asked Schultz.

"Yes," said the pig.

I ripped off my wig.

With my hair matted down I pretty near looked bald. The courtroom broke out in stitches. All the jurors smiled and laughed—one of those rare moments—even those with wigs, and Schultz and Foran suppressed smiles.

*"Your Honor, I think Mr. Rubin took off his wig," said Schultz.*

"Yes, I see he did something," Julius said.

The next day, the two most favorable jurors, Mrs. Baldwin and Kay, wore wigs to the trial and when they sat down they winked at me. It was a subversive communication. They were on our side.

I passed a note around the table telling all the other defendants about the wink. How great is the human ability for self-delusion!

They were putting me on, the yippies, fucking with my mind.

I read in the paper that longhair wigs are a booming business, especially around military bases where soldiers on leave wear wigs to hide the compulsory military short hair which they hate.

Julius's goal was to destroy our psychological balance. He knew Lennie Weinglass was young, so he deliberately kept mispronouncing Lennie's name. Weinruss, Weinstein, Feinglass. We made a sign, WEINGLASS, and held it up as a cue card when the judge began talking.

Julie said, "That may be how you do it in New York, Mr. Kunstler, but here in Chicago we do differently," playing on the jurors' Middle Western prejudice against Easterners.

*He sat on his tiptoes when Foran summed up, but when Lennie rapped, he looked to the sky and put on a charade of daydreaming.*

It was in battles with Julie that Kunstler rose to heights of dramatic greatness rarely achieved in any courtroom. Kunstler one-upped Julie and Julie gave him four years 'cause he's a fucking sore loser. He wanted Bill on hands and knees; he found himself pinned up against the wall. Bill refused to follow corrupt "professional" practices. In 99 per cent of the cases, the lawyer tells the defendants what to do. The lawyer runs the case. In our case Bill and Lennie were brothers, making decisions collectively with the defendants.

*Purpose of a lawyer is to maintain the hypocrisy of the system.* Lawyer is a court official, sworn to uphold rules of the court. Professional rules exist to protect the system at the expense of truth and justice. Professional ethics are criminal. No doctor tells on another doctor. Fuck professionals. Purpose of professional school is to prepare you psychologically to accept the system.

Each cell has a washbowl with only cold water, toilet and bunk bed. The metal door clamps shut and you are alone. Describe process when you arrive: Finger-printed, stripped of belongings, deloused in Santa Rita, fed, blood taken, catalogued, given number, put on tier.

*Lots of leisure time.*

I remember when first locked up how thrilled to find an old magazine and the Bible.

On this tier is a Muslim with a picture of Mohammed hanging on his wall, wears a Muslim cap, types all day. He's been here 23 months awaiting a trial on three murder beefs.

Each prisoner has a sad story to tell you and one after the other they can get you real down.

What political leverage do prisoners as a class have? What leverage as individuals? Judges make decisions with the D.A. symbolically looking over their shoulder. Judges live and eat in the same environment as bank presidents, police officials, politicians.

When will black prisoners get a judge of their peer?

In sitting on the bench judges think they are protecting the sacred privileges of Western society as enjoyed in the prison-like suburbs of every city.

Judges are fat creatures who rule to protect their stomach.

Stomach power!

How many judges have ever *seen* the inside of a jail? How many judges have ever spent *one night* alone behind a locked steel door?

What would have happened if Bobby Seale was driving that car in which Mary Jo Kopechne died? Would he have been strung from a tree? What if Mary Jo were driving and Teddy died? Would she ever get out of jail? THINK ABOUT IT.

**Every judge should have one qualification to be a judge: spending a year in jail.**

Every judge over black people should live in the black community, not the white suburbs.

If a defendant is found not guilty, then the prosecutor and judge should automatically be forced to serve the same jail sentence the defendant would have served had he been found guilty. Otherwise, it's not fair.

Nobody but nobody behind bars has respect for the courts, their judge, the D.A., the laws or the police. In a just society even the criminals being rehabilitated will respect the fair way they are treated.

Yes, I'm concerned for those murdered and robbed.

But it is the court system and jails which create criminals, which perpetuate murder and robbery.

Every prisoner is a political prisoner 'cause she/he is a victim of an unfair system. A lot of prisoners are in jail for stealing—I've looked in all the cells and I don't see Nelson Rockefeller in jail. A lot of prisoners are in jail for murder but I've checked each jail cell and I don't see the murderers of Fred Hampton or the Kent State and Jackson, Mississippi, students in here.

**I THINK I'M GOING BACK TO MY JAIL CELL TO MASTURBATE. BE BACK IN A MINUTE.**

The Justice Department announces that it is going after the radical left with the same methods that it went after the Mafia. Total surveillance. Get people on anything, any possible charge, taxes, dope, anything. Success of the campaign against the radical left judged by the number of heads hunted and destroyed.

Within the jails you find the peak of human emotions: hate, love, fear, bitterness, suffering. A lot of ignorance and stupidity is packed behind the walls too because one way the rulers rule is by brainwashing oppressed people and getting them to hate and fear each other.

The poor and oppressed in Amerika have been taught to believe that the poor and oppressed in other countries are their enemy, so blacks go over there to kill Viet Cong for their common enemy, the rich in Amerika.

**Tuesday, July 7**

In Alexandria a few prisoners whipped up a set of demands within minutes demanding the most human food, medical, recreational needs.

The list was smuggled out of the jail by one inmate's lawyer, mimeographed and distributed to the press. Notes were written, 16 of them, going to different tiers, spread by other prisoners on their work details. Totalitarian states, like jails, in which all information and power are controlled by the top dogs, break down when prisoners do the work and develop an informal system of communication.

In Santa Rita the mailman, a prisoner, told me there was a special hold on all my mail so the pigs could read and xerox it. So he snuck my mail to me uncensored, taking enormous risks. Prisoners learn the con mentality: do one thing while acting like you're doing another.

You don't ask too many questions while you're in jail.

You develop an underground mentality.

Supper came: we refused it. Then the word spread! The third floor didn't eat, one guy in the first tier ate, half the second tier ate. "Great, we'll get the whole jail tomorrow!" Breakfast came and went. Jails hate hunger strikes. They publicize the crimes the jails commit on the stomachs and bodies of the inmates. After breakfast the warden came over to the tier to see what was wrong. The prisoners spilled out all their grievances—half-cooked food, all starch, one slice of cheese and two slices of white bread for supper.

He kept saying, "You're right but there's nothing I can do about it. This way you're only hurting yourself." He kept nodding. I didn't say a word—I just lay in my jail cell.

Later in the morning we heard rumblings of a fight on the top tier, something about prisoners beating on a guy who insisted on crossing the strike's picket lines. And then 15 pigs appeared, lethal clubs in their right hands and tear gas canisters in their left.

I felt a rush of fear.

The pigs marched past our tier staring us down. All white, Southern. Racist. Young faces. Hungry. Hungry to use those clubs. Hungry for blood—black and hippie blood. The blacks in my tier and the Colombian about to be deported (for the third time!) grabbed broom sticks, lunch plates, anything they could get their hands on.

"All right," said the red fat flushed face of the gargantuan head pig, "everybody get in their cells but Rubin."

What! I gasped. Me! Why were they singling me out? Damn, I keep forgetting what it means to be *Jerry Rubin*! I keep forgetting my myth. The other prisoners were equally shocked; they knew I didn't cause the hunger strike. The pigs gripped their love objects, their nightsticks. The prisoners refused to go into their cells.

They looked at me.

I pictured the floors being washed with the blood of my brothers, bones breaking. I saw these young Southern redneck Virginian cops were just panting for the chance to club some black people—under the protection of law and order.

"I think you guys should go in your cells," I said. "I'll be Okay."

The pigs thundered through the door just as the prisoners moved into their cells, the little Colombian moved too slow and he got a vicious push—then the three pigs grabbed me by the pants and arms and dragged me down the corridor.

"Rubin, you're not on the outside now—here you do what we say," and threw me into a cell with a metal bed, no mattress, and the bars clanged shut.

*I was alone.*

For minutes which seemed like hours my heart pounded as I stared at the walls and heard them talk. It was one of the longest afternoons of my life. All day I heard fire engines clanging outside. The prisoners were burning paper cups, their mattresses, clothes, my tie-dye shirt, paper, magazines.

What I didn't know was that all day reporters were telephoning the jail asking about the hunger strike; their requests to tour the jail were abruptly refused—"against operations."

"How's the hunger strike going?" I kept asking a guard during the day.

"There's no hunger strike, here, Jerry. Everybody's eating."

At nine o'clock five men suddenly appeared at my cell. "All right, Jerry, get dressed, you're going."

They put a chain around me and handcuffed me, and two marshals in a new 1970 car drove me away.

"You're going to Petersburg Reformatory, Jerry, a place for youthful offenders. You'll like it there. It's like a hotel."

The attorney general of the state of Virginia personally requested to the federal marshals that I, a federal prisoner, be removed from state facilities, even though half the prisoners there are federal.

We arrived at what looked like a huge concentration camp with massive electrified fences and huge guard towers after midnight and I was stripped, searched and led through dark corridors to my cell. When I awoke in the morning I realized I was in solitary confinement, isolated from "the population," with five locked doors between me and freedom, and would be kept like this lion in a cage for the rest of the sentence.

The only "free" people you have contact with are the guards. In Petersburg the guard's main responsibility was to serve me and another young kid who passed the time all day by playing solitaire. The guard brought us breakfast at 6 A.M., lunch at 10:30, dinner at 2:30.

*"Here's your shit," he'd say. "I couldn't eat it."*

On Tuesday and Friday mornings I was allowed out of my cell to take a shower and change underwear.

Every afternoon, Monday through Friday, I got a recreation period, allowed out of my cell a half hour to walk up and down the corridor adjacent to the cell. I was filled with hate for the guard, who avoided me like the plague. He refused to communicate my messages to see my lawyer to the front office.

"When they're ready to see you, they'll come down here," he said.

He was a human being. Didn't the fact that I, another human being, was caged ever get to him? Why didn't he ever bring me a paper just to make things a bit easier? For me the day went like torture: doing time was like taking blood; as I sat alone in that cell I felt every second and minute go by—taking an eternity.

The guard was just doing his job, the silence oppressed me.

Then suddenly I was taken by pity for the guard.

What a drag!

To have a job which means you just sit watching me, serving meals and medicine, supervising daily walks! What a bore it must be. Is he any freer than I am? At least, I can read in my cell. He can't read "on the job."

The next time around I said to him, "Hey, you're just here to serve me! You're my servant!" His face boiled into a cold vicious stare and he said, "I don't serve you," then walked away. His agonized walk was the only sign of life I could see.

Around me throughout the jail I felt I was in a curious way communicating with all the jail. You can't keep a secret even in jail! Occasionally down the corridor I'd hear voices: "Jerry Rubin, how are you getting along?"

"Okay! Who are you?"

"I work in the kitchen, I'm on my way there."

"How'd you know I was here?"

*"You can't keep out the wind.* Everybody knows. We used to watch your trial every night on TV. When I was on the streets I was apathetic. But I'm not any more. If there's anything I can get you, let me know." It was a beautiful gesture, though there was nothing this prisoner could give me or do.

The first day I arrived I was marched by three paranoid guards to the third floor where a doctor checked for TB, hernia, etc. "What effect does being locked up in here have on a person, doc?" I asked.

"You should have thought about that before you came here," he said. "This isn't a pleasure dome."

The guards began marching me back. We opened a door leading to the

hallway, and there were 20 prison kitchen workers crouched on the stairway flashing me the fist and V-sign and shouting, "Power to the People! Power to the People!"

"Get out of there, you sonovabitches," shouted the guard, chasing away the vermin.

I was led back to my basement cell. But you couldn't keep out the wind.

I am lonely in isolation. I have *Die Nigger Die* by H. Rap Brown with me and I begin reading it. Rap was jailed in 1968 and kept locked up for two months in isolation while riots broke out all over Amerika after the assassination of Martin Luther King.

Rap describes his cell: "They took me to Virginia, where they put me in a

*Bobby Seale*

concentration camp near Petersburg. My cell was underground. The window looked right out on top of the grass and the only thing else I could see was this large chimney. . . . I was in a cell block by myself and between me and the outside were five locked doors."

I look up out of my cell through the window and I see the chimney!

The guard confirmed that a year ago Rap Brown was in this cell. I am in Rap Brown's old cell. All of a sudden I feel good. I have company. Rap's spirit keeps me vibrant and alive.

*Rap Brown lives.*

What enables us to take being locked up is the knowledge that so many other revolutionaries have survived long jail terms and become stronger revolutionaries. In fact, every great revolutionary has spent some time in jail. It's an occupational hazard.

While in jail I think of John Sinclair, Linda Evans, Eldridge Cleaver, Pun Plamondon, George Jackson, Tim Leary, Angela Davis, Jimmy Hoffa, Sharon Krebs, Robin Palmer, Sam Melville, all the Viet Cong behind bars, Joan Bird, Judy Clark, Huey Newton, Regis Debray, Ho Chi Minh, and all the other millions of women and men revolutionaries who survived jail.

Knowing *they* did it gives me strength.

Bobby Seale taught me something. When we arrived, the warden Moore tried to bully and intimidate Bobby. He challenged Seale to fight him. Then when I arrived he greeted me specially and ranted and raved: "There will be no press conferences here, Rubin! You are a forgotten man! This is my jail! My jail! The Panthers are Uncle Toms 'cause they let SDS run them. You think Bobby Seale can beat me? I'll fight him—or you! There will be no organizing in my jail. There are no Panthers or Stones here—there are only prisoners."

The next morning he saw Seale and me in the line with a lot of other prisoners and guards and screamed: "Hey, Bobby Seale! Jerry Rubin told me he thinks you can beat me up!" Bobby winced, then smiled. "Oh that Jerry Rubin is a crazy cat, he'd say almost anything!" Bobby had psyched Moore's ego out and he was bending with the punches.

Bobby knew his myth had preceded him: what did the warden expect the national chairman of the Black Panthers to be like?

Bobby knew what the warden's ego was like.

When the guards told Bobby to spread his cheeks, he spread his cheeks. He got handcuffed willingly; he joked and rapped with the marshals. When you are in the command of the pigs *you got to live with them*. You don't go calling them a pig no matter what you think. You develop a fake front, a jailhouse, double personality.

*Bobby Seale taught me how to do time.*

It's different when you think they are going to attack you. Che slapped the face of the Bolivian pig who was interrogating him and spit in his face. Che knew they were going to kill him anyway. It's ridiculous to provoke the pigs in jail unless you are ready to deal with their violent over-reaction.

Revolution takes place when the right wing goes after the liberals—'cause they've been so permissive and let us revolutionaries do so much shit—and the revolutionaries and the liberals join fighting fascism and the right wing.

The role of the revolutionary is to force the liberals to defend our actions, and then to fight the right wing when they go after the liberals.

I was in a bookstore in Harvard Square when someone came up to me and said, "Would you sign a copy of your book for my father?" I nodded reluctantly, with all the contradictions of being a revolutionary and a celebrity, and the ambivalence of signing autographs. But some kids like to freak out their parents.

"Okay," I said, "what's his name?" *"Eugene McCarthy."* I froze. Yippie!

In front of me stood a long-haired youth who obviously did not go Clean for Gene. Beautiful! Another wayward daughter or son from an Establishment family. What do fathers like McCarthy and Spiro do when their kids smoke dope and read dirty revolutionary books and take sworn enemies of our country as their heroes and models? It must piss them off.

Our eyes met in revolutionary comradeship.

"Thanks for the shipment of Vietnamese grass, Gene," I wrote in the book. "It was far fucking outasight!"

Wherever I go I meet governors' sons, Pentagon generals' daughters, FBI agents' kids, freak daughters and sons of the wealthiest families in Amerika, children of the ruling class, with hair all over their bodies and a stoned look in their eyes. We have infiltrated the ruling class at its most intimate level—womb of the mother and sperm of the father.

Maureen Finch told *Newsweek* that she gave her father, Robert, a copy of

*Do It!* to understand what she was thinking.

No wonder the rulers feel so desperate. How many children of the powerful are smoking dope and making bombs! Doped-up, bisexual Commie criminals have become the heroes of their kids!

### █ FREE KIM AGNEW!

I gotta admit it, I was taking a leak during what may be the most important moment in the trial. Sometimes you'd have to hold it in for hours to not miss anything.

Julius might have a heart attack any minute.

*In the quietest of moments, the laziest of days, boom!*

This was a quiet moment, a well-decorated top Chicago pig was on the stand in his uniform and medals, when I snuck into the jail lock-up toilet. I closed the door and pulled down my zipper when I could barely hear some raised voices out there and commotion. I was pissing as the voices grew to shouting and I thought: "Damn it, hurry, you're missing something." The last few drops fell into my underwear as I rushed back into the courtroom.

"What happened? What happened?" I said. Calm covered the courtroom

though Julius's neck was red and he was scowling. The pig had testified that Dave had led a violent march and Dave said, "Oh, bullshit! If you want to debate politics Okay, but don't make up things like that."

A long-haired brother in the audience stood, raised his right fist and shouted, "Right on," and as he was ejected from the courtroom, Schultz shouted: "Arrest that man!"

Dave was the bravest cat in the courtroom. He responded beautifully and spontaneously to every injustice.

You'd be sitting next to Dave in the courtroom and feel the spirit of freedom rushing through his body.

Everyone else got somewhat conditioned to the sophisticated brutality of the judicial system and managed a shake of the head or a laugh. Dave Dellinger could never condition himself to injustice. As soon as Julius the Tyrant began belittling our attorneys, Dave was on his feet, a pillar of passion and Truth. He knew the cost to him some day would be great but how could he calculate the cost to himself when the Viet Cong were shedding blood and Bobby Seale's disappearance hung over the defense table like a dark cloud?

*Dave's classic flaw is that he believes in people.*

He even believes in cops. (Dave refuses to use the word "pig.") Dave's greatest disappointment was that he was unable in five and a half months to penetrate the stone exterior of Julius Hoffman. So Dave is always getting outraged. "Who said that?" snapped Julius, picking up a quiet comment from the defense table.

"It was I, David Dellinger," said Dave, "and you oppress poor and black people."

So today as it reached 4:30 and Julie dismissed the jury but asked us to stay after school. Something was up. Julius began, "Ever since the beginning of the trial the defendant Dell—" and my heart began to pound.

To watch Dave calmly getting ready to go to jail was one of the most

*Kim Agnew!*

moving sights. He began taking important notes out of his pockets, cleaning out his briefcase, handing his phone book to his daughter Tasha. I moved to sit next to Dave and I placed my arm lovingly on his shoulder.

Julius was putting Dave in jail, canceling his bail.

They were picking us off one by one. On Friday Julius kept us after school and told us that if the defendant who spoke in Milwaukee on Friday continues to make such speeches, "I'll consider the termination of bail." "That was me," said Dave, "and I'm going to continue to speak."

That little sonovabitch. Julie was a rotten little sonovabitch. "I ask the marshals to—" All hell broke loose. Abbie heroically put himself in front of Dave and was thrown into the press section and a few marshals cuffed each other in the process. Rennie and I began shouting. The court reporter says she heard us shouting: "Bullshit! Bullshit! Take us all." Abbie blurted out, "You little runt! You're a disgrace to the Jews! You would've served Hitler better!"

Two marshals pulled Dave into the lock-up amid screaming, fighting, pushing, crying. Julius had incited a riot in his courtroom. Abbie's face showed fury. The marshals then forcibly cleared us out of the courtroom. How could we go eat supper without Dave? How could we enjoy a meal?

The trial thus entered a new stage. Julius was a madman. We went to meet at the ACLU, defendants, wives, staff.

Hayden said since Dave was a pacifist, going to jail was a natural act for him as a form of moral witness.

Abbie and I suggested we go in the courtroom tomorrow and let Julie have it to express our solidarity.

Forcing Julie to jail all of us might wake the nation up to the tyranny.

After 20 minutes the meeting broke up in anger and hate, the factions going their separate ways. Never was The Conspiracy so divided.

We felt Julius had flipped out so much that to do nothing now would make us part of his tyrannical kingdom. And besides there was Dave now sleeping in a cold Cook County Jail cell. What was a movement without solidarity?

*A movement without solidarity was a movement without soul.*

Julius's crime had to be exposed for all the world to see. Abbie, Anita, Nancy and I went to Abbie and Anita's apartment and we got really stoned, trying to decide what to do.

If all the defendants were into it, man, we could really tear up the court-room tomorrow once and for all. But if it was just Abbie and me, wouldn't it be seen as two more freaks just as Dave was a freak? We had lumps in our throats, holes at the pits of our stomachs and a dryness throughout our bodies.

We were happy, ecstatic 'cause we were involved. But the stakes were

really high.

Didn't we have a responsibility to the millions of young people out there who accepted us as models?

If we did nothing, what could we expect them to do? We were fighting an international symbolic war in that courtroom. But we couldn't decide what to do. It got late and we went our separate ways alone. We knew we had to do something, but we had no plan, no idea what to do. We'd sit back and see what happened.

That morning Dave was led into the courtroom by the marshals. The white and green band was around his right hand—the branding of each prisoner. Abbie and I sat on each side of Dave around the table like bookends. We showed him the morning clippings; friends brought Dave his juicy fat cigars.

Dave needed a shave and it was obvious he hadn't slept much. Abbie and I settled in our seats and Lennie Weinglass began his motion to the judge asking for reinstatement of bail. After Lennie uttered three sentences, Julius the Just interrupted and corrected him.

Unconsciously I felt myself rise and say, "Stop interrupting my lawyer."

"Sit down—you have a lawyer to speak for you, young man."

Dumbrowski moved to grab me.

I sat down.

Lennie began again and would you believe it! He said something the judge didn't want to hear and the judge interrupted him again.

Again I was on my feet. "Stop interrupting my lawyer. Let him continue."

The marshals were on me.

The dam broke loose.

For the next hour Abbie and I, bookends around Dave, took turns letting Julius hear the feelings in our hearts. One of us would react and the marshals would move to shut him up while the other would pick it up. We were angry. We were beside ourselves. We were overbrimming with revolutionary heat.

*"Stick it up your bowling ball, Julie."*

"Every kid in the world hates you. You are the laughing stock of the world."

*"How many blacks eat at the Standard Club, Julie?"*

"Your name is synonymous with Adolf Hitler in the world today!"

And then Abbie hit Julius with the loudest line of the trial:

**"SHANDA FOR THE GOYEM!"**

Which, loosely translated, means: "Front Man for the Wasp Power Structure!"

Finally we were expressing what we really felt about Julius. Every chicken reporter and spectator in the room loved it—we were expressing the words and feelings that were in everyone's heart. We were saying what everyone was scared shitless to say. We were telling the tyrant off. It was the wildest verbal barrage in the history of the trial, even surpassing Bobby Seale who only called Julie a "pig." Tension filled the room: you could cut it with a knife. People held their breath. It was one of the most intense moments of truth in the courtroom.

Julius sat there leering, glaring, his eyes raging with hate.

We told the marshals off. "Lay off, Ron." There was Dumbrowski—in the halls he smiled, said "Hi Rubski," real buddy-buddy like; in the courtroom he became Julius's executioner. Everyone expected Julius to jail us any minute. Just as quiet settled we were off again. The jury was brought in and the trial resumed.

Julius denied the motion without hearing any argument.

He ordered Lennie to sit down.

Bill was on his feet—the marshals forcibly sat him down. As Julius was to leave the courtroom our cries of "Tyrant!" rang in his ears.

We went to a press conference where we castigated the press for just sitting in the courtroom as machines watching fascism go by and doing nothing but taking notes.

"They could shoot us bloody in the courtroom and you'd do nothing," I said, tears in my eyes. In the hallways the reporters all told us how sick and awful Julius was, how brave we were—in the courtroom they became lambs. Oh, those reporters were giants in the shower! In the courtroom they were afraid of losing their jobs.

What would be the impact if the reporter for the *New York Times* or CBS TV stood up to say his piece too?

But all the reporters were frozen in their inhuman roles.

*Observers.*
*Observers.*

Throughout the whole trial during all the bullshit never once did a reporter break the media of the courtroom. They just sat there in their front-row seats with fat, satisfied, frightened liberal faces watching the zoo: look at the vultures eating human flesh.

*Judge Hoffman and Colleagues*

They acted out their rebellion by refusing to speak to the prosecutors. But really it was the prosecution which spurned them. Foran and Schultz only spoke to three or four reporters, the most conservative. At the end of each trial day the Chicago *Tribune* reporter went over to the prosecution table to rap.

The prosecutor refused to speak to the *New York Times* or CBS. They agreed with Spiro, saw them as part of our team.

The courtroom was full of liberals writing books and articles on the trial totally supporting the defendants. They were *for* us, but not *with* us. It was weird relating to them, and I could not hide the contempt I felt for them, no

matter how sympathetic they were to the "revolution." To them it was "entertainment" or "enlightenment"—never life or death.

The participant always has some contempt for the sympathetic observer, especially when your life is at stake.

Revolutionary media voyeurs are a drag, forever dishonestly chasing after their own identity.

The liberal press supported us—but so what? We had no doubt that once we were off in jail, the liberals would utter a sigh of cosmic tragedy, give a few conscience bucks, go back to their middle-class prisons and move on to the next circus.

For the same actions around Dellinger, I got sentenced by Julius to a year in jail for contempt and Abbie got 12 days. My performance was equal to Abbie's. Julie had a double standard.

The last place you'll find fairness is in a federal courtroom.

The court system satirizes itself.

*In the coolest move of the trial Abbie renounced his last name 'cause he didn't want to be associated with Julius Hoffman.*

*"I don't use that name any more," Abbie said. "You destroyed it."*

### Wednesday, July 8

I was invited to Los Angeles to do a series of TV shows. Top was the Regis Philbin Show, Joey Bishop's ex-sidekick. When I arrived the first person I saw was a historical relic. But there he was in flesh and blood, *Pat Boone!*

I spread the Viet Cong flag out on the table for decoration—anything to get Pat Boone's blood a'boiling—and kept an American flag on my seat just to keep Regis uptight. "What are you going to do with that?" he kept asking.

In the 1950's Pat Boone was the symbol of Good Amerikan youth, and his clean white bucks symbolized Amerika.

Remember Pat? He'd never kiss girls in the movies.

Before the show started Pat told me that that was all a publicity gimmick. This was one of those shows, a wild free-swinging affair, that the viewers of L.A. never saw. It was too hot and the station head decided to kill it.

The VC flag on the table, and my telling Pat Boone that Christianity has murdered more people than any other ism in the history of the world—he kept trying to give me this pornographic paperback called *Torture for Christ*, about some priest who supposedly was in a Communist jail—was too much for the station big wigs to handle.

I went to Cleveland to do an interview show with Dorothy Fuldheim, Cleveland's oldest interviewer, and the battleax flipped out. I said "Pigs," and she said, "Are you referring to policemen or animals?" I said, "Pigs, I mean policemen."

"I love the police," she screamed.

"I love the Black Panthers!" I screamed back.

With that she grabbed my book, heaved it halfway across the room and stopped the taping.

"Get off my show, you uncouth beast!"

*I dug her.*

Schultz's wife showed up for court one day with their two beautiful daughters. One said, "I came to see Abbie." Stew and Nancy cooked up an idea of playing on Mrs. Schultz's *Jewish guilt.*

Nancy went up to her and said, "Do you understand any Yiddish?" Mrs. Schultz nodded. Then Nancy said, "What your husband is doing is a shanda for the goyem. Do you know what that means?"

"Yes I do," said a red-faced Mrs. Schultz, walking away, in anger.

Calling Julius a "shanda for the goyem" exposes another reality of the courtroom: *a Jewish morality play*—Julius is Jewish—in fact, he was the B'nai B'rith Man of the Year. The yippies in The Conspiracy—me, Abbie, Lee—were Jewish, which is not to say that only Jews can be yippies, although yippie is very Jewish. Both our lawyers, Lennie and Bill, are Jewish. The only Jew on the jury, a little brown-haired woman, was for acquittal and she was the last juror to hold out.

The hard-driving, conscientious prosecutor, Schultz, who made our indictment and conviction his passion, is Jewish.

We knew that Jews are an oppressed minority—murdered, jailed and ostra-

cized across the world for 2,000 years.

But Schultz went after us with all the fanaticism of a Nazi prosecutor upholding law and order.

We kept reminding Julius that everything done to the Jews in Nazi Germany was legal. Judges in black robes committed crimes in the name of the State.

*Do Jews become free when they put on those black robes and become those judges? Or become prosecutors for the state?*

Here was Jewish Schultz doing all the work for Foran, a Catholic, and his political ambitions, and helping clear the political grudges of Mayor Daley, an anti-Semite.

Somewhere, somehow, we tried to reach Julius and Schultz on the only thing we had in common with them: our historical Jewishness, the role of the oppressed in history.

Was there a victim, an oppressed person, somewhere beneath that exterior of hanging judge and vicious prosecutor?

Throughout the whole trial I took as my personal project the educating of Schultz. I respected him 'cause he was a damn good prosecutor and knew what we were about. He knew we were revolutionaries. I dug his fantasies.

But Schultz was working for racist, anti-Semitic cops, who are capable of putting black people in concentration camps. Jews betray their own oppression when they help the oppressors.

Schultz and Julius Hoffman are working for racist pigs who will try to put millions of young Jewish radicals and hippies before firing squads.

I kept sitting next to him (our tables were adjacent) and saying to him, loud enough so he'd hear but not loud enough to disrupt the trial, "Schultz, you would have made a great Nazi prosecutor." It didn't work. Schultz didn't even crack a sympathetic look. Every so often Schultz would wise to the judge that I was attacking his "religion."

In his famous post-trial speech before the Boosters Club of his son's high-school football team, Foran said he was surprised Schultz didn't haul off and punch me.

It is the Jew who should always be on the side of the poor, the oppressed, the underdog, the wretched of the earth, because of the Jewish experience. And thousands of young ex-Amerikan ex-Jews are. Three of the kids killed at Kent State were Jews. An unusually high proportion of hippies and revolutionaries are Jews. Amerikan Jews are losing their kids at a faster rate than any other religious or social group 'cause young Jews are becoming hippies and yippies.

I personally feel very torn about being born Jewish.

I know it made me feel like a minority or outsider in Amerika from my birth and helped me become a revolutionary. I am shocked at Julius Hoffman

and Richard Schultz 'cause they try to be so Amerikan. Don't they know they're still "Jewish" no matter how much "power" or "security" in Amerika they have?

When I was in Germany recently I felt very Jewish. Stew and I freaked out when we saw a German in uniform, even a ticket-taker on the train! Even Brian *Flanagan* said he felt Jewish! We met Danny Cohn-Bendit who now lives in Frankfurt. We said to Danny, "Hey we thought the subway conductor was taking us to a concentration camp," and Danny jumped up and down and shouted, "Me too! I feel the same way!"

But despite this, two experiences helped me become a Communist revolutionary. One was working as a reporter on a newspaper in Cincinnati and seeing how unhappy everyone there was. The second was living for one and a half years in Israel and reacting against the capitalism, racism and Imperialism there.

Judaism no longer means much to us because the Judao-Christian tradition has died of hypocrisy. Jews have become landlords, businessmen, judges and prosecutors in Amerika. I do not believe in "freedom" for Jews at the ex-

pense of Arabs and black people. **I think we must destroy all sectarian religions to create a common Communist humanity based on a universal morality.**

At the end of the trial I received the following letter: "Rubin, it is Jews like you who will make people put Jews like me in the ovens." The concentration camp fear of Jews has made them rush to prove themselves to Pig Amerika, and make themselves "secure" with money and property.

But it is a false security, a competitive security in a country built on the blood and tears of the oppressed.

Judaism—as well as Christianity and other religions—have universalized into yippie.

We will not raise our kids to be Jewish or any other "ish."
*If Moses were alive today, he'd be an Arab guerrilla.*

The white race can only save itself by condemning its own history and

*... Arab guerrillas*

looking at the world from the point of the people it has oppressed. Our parents may not be able to do this, but we can. We do this not out of guilt—we do this because we want to be free ourselves.

We ended up with a jury of ten women and two men. That was deliberate. We systematically threw men off the jury 'cause they are ideological and honky, and we preferred women, who are more human and empathetic, and who have less material stake in the system.

We looked at the jury as a jury of our mothers. *We felt Mother might forgive, while Father would punish.*

Because of the male supremacist views of both the women and men on the jury, the women chose one of the two men as foreman. Both men ended up voting for a sentence of immediate death by firing squad. Some of the women wanted acquittal but they weren't strong enough to hold out against the pressure of Julius Hoffman, the marshals, and "the system."

We considered a massive demonstration at the Palmer House demanding "Free the Jury!" The jury was locked up and we were free. We vehemently opposed the locking up of the jury. We even wanted them to be able to read newspapers and watch TV. After all, the jury still had its prejudices—they were locked up in their hotels with the same prejudices they began the trial with.

Some of the things they weren't supposed to do were idiotic.

After every court session, morning and afternoon, Julie warned them not to discuss the trial with anyone, not even among themselves. Now what else did these jurors have in common but our trial? They used to argue about how to bring up their children—which was just another way of discussing the trial—

"Would you want your kids to grow up and be like them?" the right-wing piggy jurors were quoted as saying.

Who in their right mind believed that the jurors were not discussing the case among themselves?

After court sometimes we'd see the jury bus and wave at them and then get so excited. "Kay waved at me." "Mrs. Fritz really gave me a fantastic smile!" "Even Mrs. Wallace was friendly."

We had nicknames for all the jurors. The most important juror, in fact, the most important person in the courtroom, was Mrs. Baldwin. That's not her real name but on the day of jury selection she walked past the defense and prosecution table and to the jury box carrying a book by James Baldwin. Each one of us at the table did a triple take when we saw her and the book.

*A juror who reads!*

*A juror who reads James Baldwin!*

We closed the jury as soon as we could to keep Mrs. Baldwin and from then on our entire court strategy, with its overoptimistic strategy, was based on Mrs. Baldwin on the jury.

Yippie intelligence agents brought back the info that Mrs. Baldwin was a dyed-pink liberal, supporter of Women for Peace, anti-war advocate, even a marcher. Newspaper excerpts quoted Foran as saying the defense had a "rock" on the jury.

From then on no conversation ever took place about the trial that did not put Mrs. Baldwin as the central focus.

Every single one of us believed a hung jury was inevitable.

Mrs. Baldwin would never let us down. She would never put us at the mercy of that wicked judge. Watch Mrs. Baldwin in the courtroom. She'd actually give me the V-sign when the judge wasn't looking—not the clenched fist, I admit, but at least a V.

Julius's actions would have her gasping. She loved our literary and artistic witnesses. We brought Mailer to the stand so he'd write a book about the trial (he didn't) and for Mrs. Baldwin. If we could have located James Baldwin, we'd have brought him to the box. We'd have found some reason.

Mrs. Baldwin laughed at the right places, sneered at the right places, looked bored at the right moments. And then the clincher: Rennie was giving a speech at some Illinois college when a hippie young woman raised her hand and said to 2,000 people, "Don't worry, my mother's on the jury and she'll never find you guilty. She told me the government hasn't proved a thing."

*Her mother was Mrs. Baldwin.*

The daughter then began attending the trial, sitting in the front row and waving and smiling and rooting for us, and waving to her mother. How could Mrs. Baldwin find us guilty and still speak to her daughter?

Our next favorite juror was the youngest member of the jury, Kay Richards, who sat next to Mrs. Baldwin and was real chummy with her.

She was twenty-three.

Look at the seductive, romantic way she looks at us. We were taken in. She fed our male egos. We even fantasized that after the trial we'd be turning Kay on to LSD and maybe even Molotov cocktails.

On the other side were Mrs. Daley and Mrs. Wallace, two pigs who sat in the first row and spent the whole trial leering and sneering at us; the wino with the new suit; a middle-aged black woman who wore a red-haired wig; assorted other Average Amerikans, with maybe a chance at a few of them being sleepers and supporting Mrs. Baldwin.

Who could tell?

For five and a half months these human beings sat in their chairs and watched the most exciting theater in town without ever so much as changing a facial expression.

How do human beings turn themselves into such automatons?

It was wild to watch Mr. Kratzke doze off and see Mrs. Peterson keep shaking him up. A number of jurors slept through most of the trial. Except for Mrs. Baldwin, Kay and the two pigs, the rest of the jurors reacted to nothing. We nicknamed one woman "the dead woman" and asked Kunstler to make a motion asking for an autopsy on her.

*"Your Honor, would you please check the second woman in the second row? We think she may have expired."*

I looked at the jury and saw two Amerikas: basically, Mrs. Baldwin versus the rest. The same issues would be fought in the jury room that were fought in the courtroom.

It was artists and writers and students and singers versus policemen.

Humanistic Amerika versus racist, ignorant, repressive Amerika. C'mon, Mrs. Baldwin, fight on! Your battle may be the most important of all.

*One of the raging issues of the trial was where the defendants could pee and shit.* At first we got a "privilege"—being able to leave the courtroom to use the bathroom in the hall. It was like being in kindergarten. If too many defendants were out of the room, the prosecutor would tattle-tale to the

teacher (Julie) and the trial would stop until we returned. Soon whenever we left, a marshal would follow us out to watch where we went. If we went to make a phone call, the marshal would tattle to the teacher.

The marshals discovered that being yippies, give us an inch, we take a mile.

In a totalitarian society the toilet is a center of free activity. You can do a lot of things giving the toilet as a reason. We'd even sneak down to other courtrooms to freak out other judges.

Finally Julius kept us after school to tell us that we could no longer leave the courtroom but now could use the lock-up adjacent to the courtroom. It was a humiliating blow.

A john with bars!

We thought of stopping up the toilet and then rushing into the courtroom, "Your Honor, I ran out of toilet paper!"

We were on our way to jail. The noose around our neck. The next day I was kidding Schultz when he looked at me, smiled triumphantly, and said quietly, "Why don't you go to the bathroom?" pointing to the lock-up toilet.

"I'd rather do it on you," I said quietly, then I jumped to my feet, tattle-tale-like, and I said, "Your Honor, Mr. Schultz just told me to go to the jail bathroom, as if it's some victory to make us go to the bathroom in the jail."

Schultz shrugged up to the podium, "Yes, Your Honor, I succumbed. I said that. I'm sorry. But these defendants have been harassing police and other authorities for several years now, and I lost my temper. But after I said that, Rubin said he'd rather 'do it' on me."

We were reeling on the table, laughing. Another day in the federal court in Chicago, the *highest* court in the land.

After the prosecution finished its case we debated what to do. I wanted to put on a defense to last years. What a way to tie up the courts! We'd put on the stand everyone *who came* to the demonstration to say why they came.

Everyone, Everyone, Everyone.

We'd also put on the stand everyone *who didn't come* to Chicago to say why they didn't come.

The lawyers told us that every lawyer and legal expert near the trial felt the government had not proved a thing and we should not put on a defense. By that time haggling within the defendants reached such a point that we seriously considered stopping.

Dave leaned to stopping.

Tom wanted a tight, narrow case.

Abbie and I wanted a circus.

We couldn't settle it through debate. We decided to settle it day by day, week by week. We couldn't agree on a strategy so we'd all bring our kind of witness in. The yippie strategy was to bring our way of life into the courtroom in the hopes of turning on the jury. If we failed, at least we'd have fun. We wanted to see our friends on the witness stand. Lenny Bruce once said

he'd like to do his act before the Supreme Court. If they laughed, he'd be not guilty. We couldn't do our Festival of Life in Lincoln Park; maybe we could do it in the courtroom.

*Our chief witness would be Pigasus.*

The plane arrived in Minneapolis and the passengers, weary businessmen, executives, salesmen, started filing out. The oppressed stewardesses stood at the door forced to be mannequin-like, flashing automatic smiles and "good-bye's." They are fired if they don't smile and say good-bye to every passenger.

On the outside I could hear an uproar, wild applause, screaming and boom! there at the end of the corridor were packed in 300 painted faces, smiling, cheering, playing tambourines, harmonicas, drums, flutes, kazoos, singing and giving each departing passenger from the plane a hero's greeting.

As each passenger appeared, a wild cheer arose from the crowd.

"She's here!"

"He's here!"

"Where's the celebrity?"

"Who's the celebrity?"
*"You're the celebrity!"*

At first the businessmen were annoyed—with schedules to make, figures to remember, anxieties to keep—they don't like the dull rhythm of Amerikan society disturbed.

But what are you to do when there are 300 happy, screaming, freaky people welcoming you as if you're a conquering war hero, championship football team?

Pretty soon even the businessmen were over their embarrassment and smiling.

The yippies had taken over the Minneapolis airport. Liberate the airports! A few uniformed pigs were around but nothing illegal was going on—except happy people and fun.

The merry pranksters pranced down the long corridors dancing and filling the place with music. Clown hats, bright costumes, pot, free cookies for all. Soon the yippies were in their cars and buses and off. The yippies were gone and suddenly a deep quiet fell over the airport. Function took over again but people would be talking about it for weeks.

I felt like telling a witness or Schultz or Julius, "Damn good acting job, Julie!" One moment of trial came close to that. Julie read the indictment to the assembled jurors with emphasis, passion, sincerity, power. Like he believed in his act and our guilt. Startled, we looked at each other and Kunstler rose to interrupt Julie.

"Your speaking would do Orson Welles proud," said Kunstler.

Julie reddened, then leered. "Why, Mr. Kunstler, how nice of you to say that."

We heard that Julie ate at the Standard Club, a 100-year-old German-Jewish members-only exclusive club across the street from the Federal Building. Marshals chaperoned Julie there and then picked him up and brought him back to the court building.

One morning at lunch recess, Bill's eyes were popping as he called Abbie and me over. *"We're going to eat lunch with the judge today,"* Bill winked. "Let's go."

A long line of Conspiracy personalities began marching toward the Standard Club. "How'd we get this?" I posed to Bill, and he smiled again, threw his

arm around me, and said something about an invitation from a member who likes us. There we were, kids on an expedition into another world, me, Nancy, Abbie, Bill, Lotte, Jules Feiffer, Dave, Jason Epstein, Tony Lukas, Norman Mailer, Saul Alinsky.

I kept thinking to myself: "What is Julie going to think when he sees us enter his private safe world, his pure world, where he escapes from the rabble? But the rabble can be anywhere in Amerika.

"This might do it.

"This might be enough to give him that heart attack."

We reached the club to hear some crushing news—you had to have a tie and sports coat to enter. I rushed down the street into the nearest haberdashery and said, "Give me the two cheapest ties you got!" I could use my winter coat for a sports coat, but Abbie had no coat. He went into a barber shop and in a second emerged with a coat.

But then came the next crisis: the Standard Club was a male-only establishment. Nancy and Lotte Kunstler couldn't enter. I was really heartbroken. Some of the fun went out of the escapade. So, angrily, Nancy and Lotte wrote on the door, "Male chauvinist pigs!" and left.

We got in the elevator to freak out Julius. There it was—a large dining hall with many tables and white tablecloths and black waiters and many old men hunched over and we said, "Where is he? Let's get a table near him," and someone said, "Look, there he is in the back at the right," and I saw Julie in a suit and he was looking our way red-faced and shocked and leaped up and moved a table away.

We had to split in two groups and Abbie and I—I bet he never thought he'd ever see us with ties on!—picked out a table near Julius and we kept giving him the V-sign and smiling broadly.

The rest of the place tried to pretend nothing unusual had happened but damn! up went Julie again and this time he sat in a chair behind this pillar.

We moved our seats so we could keep a smiling eye on him.

As Julie left after eating he stopped at table after table shaking hands, a hero among his own kind, and disappeared. We heard later that Julie arranged with waiters to serve us coffee just as he was leaving to avoid a direct confrontation.

It was psychological guerrilla warfare.

Julie must know he is safe nowhere.

*We appear on his TV all the time so he stopped watching TV.*
*We appear all over his papers so he stopped reading the papers.*
*We appear all over his streets so he stopped walking the streets.*
Now we had invaded the place where he thought he was safe—his eating place. Where would we strike next?

Back in the courtroom Abbie and I kept our ties on and giggled all afternoon while Julie kept scowling.

Weeks later we read that the Standard Club unearthed the member who invited us—a young guy who inherited his membership from his father, what else—and severely reprimanded him, deciding not to kick him out of the club.

Working on the paranoia and fear of the enemy is our secret weapon.

**We've got to destroy TV.** Carry your TV's in front of CBS and NBC and smash them to bits. TV is chewing gum for the mind. TV turns human beings into spectators and passive receivers.

Since we were reared on hamburgers and television, we know how important TV is for the pacification of the population. We yippies try to use TV time to shock the sleeping viewers into attention. We are obnoxious on TV, obscene, violent, horrible, contemptible, immoral.

I wondered whether or not to go on the Dick Cavett Show. I couldn't take part in the "How are you" friendly pat-on-the-back cocktail party chatter characteristic of late nite shows. Now we have a juggler, then a dancing group, then a movie star, then a skier, then a revolutionary.

"So how's the rev biz, Jer?"

That would be a counterrevolutionary situation. All words could be co-opted. Just *talking* in that format might be counterrevolutionary.

Whatever I did had to be nonverbal, visual: to be revolutionary we had to break the format of the show. It would be nothing for the content to be revolutionary.

The war is immoral.

Blah Blah Blah. Everything has been said. The show's format reduces all statements to mashed potatoes. *"Armed struggle" sounds like a detergent.* Mediocrity is built in.

Walking onto the stage in these shows is entering a strange artificial world. The lights glare at you. The show is taped at 6 P.M. even though shown later at night. The audience is out there, filled with people from rural Amerika who wrote away for tickets months earlier. Freaks are ushered up to the third balcony. And there's Cavett, shitting in his pants, with a long list of prepared questions in front of him.

The compulsion on all these shows is to be nice, be nice, don't get angry, don't raise your voice, don't be violent; cool, calm conversation will settle all, above all be entertaining. Ain't these revolutionaries cute? My style would have to be revolutionary. The medium is the message.

I war-painted my face and wore judge's robes. When Cavett offered me a martini, I tore the robes in half and mixed my drink with the shreds.

Abbie went on the Merv Griffin Show wearing a shirt made out of the Amerikan flag. Just before Abbie's appearance the president of CBS got on TV and explained that Mr. Hoffman had violated the laws of several states by wearing the shirt and CBS would use electronic means to save the viewer from seeing the shirt.

What then happened was the electronic nightmare, *electronic fascism.*

Watching it I actually got scared, frightened. Every time Abbie talked the screen was total black darkness. When Griffin and Abbie rapped to each other the screen showed Griffin talking to a half-black screen.

Abbie's right-wing "balance" person kept saying over and over again, "It's a free country. Look, Abbie, Amerika can't be *that* bad if it lets you on TV," all the while speaking to a blank screen.

Forcing the pigs to censor your body is so much more revolutionary than forcing them to censor your words.

We have to liberate TV for the people and take it away from the control creeps. We need our own TV stations and our own means of information and mental freedom. Then, after yippies take over TV, other yippies will blow up all the TV stations so that people begin to look, talk and be with each other again.

Fuck electronic control!

The media control our consciousness. As revolutionaries we must know and use the media. But we must not become bastards of the media. Reality exists on TV and on the streets. Unfortunately what most people believe is what's on TV.

That's why we must be both media and armed street guerrillas.

It's really true. *It didn't happen if it wasn't on TV.* Truth exists in images. A lot of armed struggle will take place on TV.

Revolutionaries must use the media to destroy the media.

Revolutionaries must pick up the gun to put down the gun.

## SELF-AWARENESS IS TRUTH.

## THE MEDIA PREVENT SELF-AWARENESS.

Amerika's TV newsmen and personalities are little more than scared mothers and fathers. I came to Washington to do an interview with Martin Agronsky. Poor Martin. He was so worried. Concerned. Anxious. *What do you want,* Jerry? What do you *really want?*

Amerika is having ulcers 'cause its kids do not want *the best* Amerika can offer them. We are copping out of the rat race. Don't you think the fact that Walter Cronkite's daughter lives a hippie existence on a distant Hawaiian island affects Walter's coverage of the news at night?

Amerika expects black people to reject it. But its own kids? No, no, heavens, no! This kind of rejection is the biggest insult of all.

So they try to interpret us as just another fad. But in their hearts they know. We are never coming home.

Martin looked at me sadly and said about *Do It!*: "No, I didn't understand your book, Jerry. *How can I understand your book when I don't understand my own son?"*

We have deserted their sinking ship.

Deep down they know their kids are right: they are miserable and unsatisfied. They built their world out of material goals and it means nothing.

We are free—doing what they wish they could do.

I did a morning TV interview show with Joseph Smith. On TV Joe was serious, probing, not hostile, but skeptical. I was so "idealistic." Aren't people naturally selfish? "Who would work if everything is free?"

On the way out after the interview I stopped off at the CBS john, *where I was followed by two CBS house pigs who trailed me right into the stall.* (The New York bomb scare strikes deep.)

93

From there Joe and I went to an apartment where we smoked the best Commie grass that Amerikan GI's smoke. Our masks fell off and our souls lay bare. Joe, the TV personality, said, "I'm not happy. What am I but a voice announcer? We're all unhappy, getting drunk during the day. Tell me, tell me, what can we do?"

Did I—freak, revolutionary, convicted criminal felon—have any solutions?
They are bored—and boredom is the Amerikan disease, as common as the
cold. They are not creative. I suggested to Joe that tomorrow while doing his
show live he say, "Ladies and gentlemen, Fuck, *Fuck, FUCK!*" The shock
throughout Middle Amerika would be volcanic: he would go down in *history*.

Joe shriveled up. "No, no, I can't do that. I'd lose my job. I still do *some* good."

The middle-class neurosis of fear, insecurity and boredom had defeated this grown six-foot man.

Dramatic alternatives were beyond his psychological comprehension. "No, I can't. I can't. Well, I guess I'm not really a yippie."

The Amerikan middle class dies on.

Nobody can break out of her or his role.

To be called a clown in Amerika is an insult. But we are all clowns, fools, goof-offs, dreamers, children. Everyone is scared people won't take them "seriously."

We've got to die so we can be reborn. We got to jump out of our roles and change costumes. We gotta stop taking ourselves so damn seriously!

We gotta be what we always wanted to be, do what we've always wanted to do. We gotta change our lives and be kids again.

Every few years we should change our personalities, houses, jobs completely and start our lives all over again. Life should always be full of abrupt new beginnings.

Free bubble gum after the revolution for everyone.

Shock! Do the forbidden. As Abbie says, "Break every law, including the law of gravity."

*If everyone did what she or he wanted to do, we'd have a revolution in Amerika in one hour!*

I want to do TV commercials for grass after the revolution. Or just roll joints all day and listen to Dylan.

I went to CBS to meet Walter Cronkite. Walter could announce the end of the world and you'd believe it.

"Walter," I wanted to tell him, "we are going to let *you* announce the victory of the revolution."

Walter must be conscious of himself as an actor, a great actor. I virtually embraced him. He smiled. Walter seemed slightly touched by my enthusiasm for him: politics aside, here was one actor (me) paying him, another actor, a real compliment.

"Watch out, Walter," I said. "Spiro is going to get you."

I told him that the right wing sees him as the enemy 'cause he's the permissive parent promoting our misbehavior on national TV.

Then Walter blew my mind. Waving good-bye and shaking my hand, he said, *"When the Nazis come to my door, I hope you guys are going to be outside on the barricades."*

It was a good-bye knuckle-ball comment, stated as light as a feather, knocking me off my feet.

Family crisis: running out of rolling paper.

Worse family crisis: running out of matches.

"If you can't be with the one you love, love the one you're with."

The Conspiracy 8 Trial had been a national schoolroom. Millions of young kids saw themselves sitting in that courtroom—and Julius became Every Judge, Every Pig, Every Authority Figure, Every Teacher, Every Parent.

Thanks to the technology of the media, *nothing is local any more.*

Local and national issues merge.

We don't break the windows of Telegraph Avenue in Berkeley because we have revolutionary grievances against the petty capitalists: and every splattered window on Telegraph is also a blow against President Nixon, the FBI and capitalism.

The Bank of America in Santa Barbara is the perfect symbol: the bank represents direct oppression of Latin Americans and black people, direct symbol of the Amerikan Greed, while at the same time it is a wart, a cyst, a malignant tumor in the body of *our community* imposed *from the outside.*

Riots are emotional expressions for self-determination by oppressed peoples.

You cannot vote or petition the Bank of America out of your community or out of existence: the only alternative is a Molotov cocktail or dynamite. Students, nonstudents, hippies, women, Weatherpeople, gays, yippies—young people—are an oppressed people living within Imperialism, living on campuses controlled from the outside.

Is there any doubt that we must first destroy the existing Imperialist structures in order to build our own?

In riots, in battles with police, in overthrowing unrepresentative, foreign control, we are writing the history of our generation in the streets and becoming liberated men and women.

### Thursday, July 9

It had been a relatively quiet winter. The columnists were "dreaming" about the pacification of the campuses. But the movement always moves in a schizophrenic curve—up and down, high and low. During the low periods, wounds are being healed, forces massed and energy harnessed for the coming high. We know that intellectually, but we get depressed anyway during low periods when we see friends battling, sisters and brothers bad-rapping each other, heavy factionalization. Periods of community low are the sum total of thousands of individual depressions. The community crisis creates individual crises—or individual crises mount to a community crisis.

No individual can escape the mood of his or her generation. We live in one of those periods of history, including rapid change, where *the history of the movement is the history of each individual.*

Tell me where the Berkeley movement is on the up-down curve and I'll tell you how all my friends are doing personally. All individual problems, however private, are group problems. That should give us comfort. It means we've got a lot of company.

It is almost a certain fact of the scientific curve of the movement that a few months after the "up" virtually everyone except the perpetual optimists—I am a perpetual optimist—would be putting down the "up," expressing defection and disillusionment, his or her mood bathed in cynicism, with fierce attacking going on.

● *Today's leaders will be next month's scapegoats.*

All the depression, emotional bloodletting, hurt feelings then disappear in a second with the next crisis, battle and community experience.

Riots, campus struggles, demonstrations—the longer, the better—are social, community orgies, group celebrations. All the factions love each other. Heroism comes from the unlikeliest quarters. Strangers greet one another on the street. Everyone is a sister and brother, a comrade, in the struggle. Chemistry students work with English students.

**Rallies are parties.**

Building seizures are communal living experiences.

The boredom, the meaningless competition, the isolation is over. We are an *army*. We feel the solidarity of guerrilla *soldiers*. We lose our own ego in the collective ego. We're lucky! We are fighting for our community, our turf, our land.

"We" are "Berkeley," "we" are "Isla Vista," "we" are "the people."

Every year marks the evolution of the revolution so the revolution moves in stages of growth of the collective unconscious: from civil rights marches to student demonstrations to peace protesters to hippie to yippie to street fighters to guerrillas—this is one curve of our past 11 years. Our evolution responds to *our* experience and the impact of external events on us.

We change costumes, language and rules as history moves.

Young kids today will not have to repeat the steps and roles we made: many young kids are freaks from birth, take dope at an early age and experience no culture other than the freak culture.

Radicalism does not proceed step by step, logically or rationally: radicalism is an insight, a historical explosion with body and mind, an Apocalypse, in which individuals change themselves overnight.

Historical experience is not an intellectual experience. The mind is lost in a spiritual orgasm, adventure: *becoming a revolutionary is like falling in love.* No one can "explain" it, no warning is given, and the causes are cataclysmic.

There must have been acid in the drinking water of 1968, because 1969-70 saw radicalizing everywhere.

The Democrats at the convention and the dramatic Acting Out of the failure of rational, moral, honest McCarthy proved something to people who didn't even personally experience it.

The 1968 election and demonstration were a Historical Theater for thousands to change from. The crowds at radical rallies went from 500 to 3000, 4000, 10,000. Everybody saw it: "Last year in my law school I knew all the radicals, I could count them. But this year there are so many, I can't count them."

The same in business schools, medical, everywhere.

The number of stoned freaks quadrupled: from a mere handful to hundreds, thousands. And among young kids, the straight left was dead, everyone was a freak.

You didn't have to go to Berkeley any more—Berkeley came to you, Berkeley was everywhere.

From September to March we all observed these changes dramatically but they were the bottom of the iceberg. On the surface things were quiet. It was even still LBJ's war that Nixon was still trying to manage.

Then boom! The trial ended. The unbelievable happened—we actually went to jail. Nobody believed it would happen. The iceberg emerged. A thousand riots broke out across the USA—from the bottom up! And that was the beginning of guerrilla war as Ohio State, Santa Barbara, Seattle, Berkeley, Buffalo, Southern Illinois State—of all places!—blew up. A human volcano was bursting and it could not be stopped.

Our trial was merely the excuse: if it were not our trial, it would have been something else.

We sat in locked jail cells on the "hole" tier of Cook County and we knew we were going to be free: the only way to "stop" the riots—even temporarily—was by freeing us. In jail we would be explosive political prisoners, a festering sore on Amerika's ass.

The defendants sat around a table watching TV and debated the "credit" for the riots. "Seattle, that's me," I cheered, "I spoke there." "So did I," said Hayden. "I did the one at Madison." "I spoke at Ann Arbor." The convicted riot inciters kidded each other about actually causing the riots, but we knew who had caused them.

Credit where it is due.

*Julius Hoffman incited the riots.*

Scene: The Courtroom. Empty. The jury has gone home to its poodles, soap operas and color TV's. They'd done their *Amerikan duty*. Julie was already packing for his vacation in Florida.

The courtroom was completely empty—lovers, relatives, friends, spectators barred—Anita's words, "We'll dance on your grave, Julie," still ringing from the walls. "Why, just the last time we were in court my life was threatened," said Julie—paranoid to the end—defending the law. It was the ultimate cruelty.

We were going to serve our jail sentence without our dearest friends being present. We were going to be sentenced to jail in an empty courtroom: full only with press. To add vengeance to injury there in the front row with lean, hungry, satisfied looks on their faces sat three members of the Chicago Red Squad.

Our fury grew.

*Our enemy could see us in our final day but not our friends and lovers.*

This moment—the moment of truth—was the moment spared from the eyes of the jurors. They would not have to see the results and consequences of their actions. It should be made compulsory for all jurors to witness the moment of sentencing. We asked that the Red Squad be removed. They were.

It was the moment Julie was waiting for. Unfortunately the maximum he could give us was five years. But despite the frigid, empty, cold environment—despite the absence of our friends' beautiful faces, despite the final victory of Julius—jail for us—this was to be *our* day.

Before sentencing, each of us was permitted a final statement.

We all had lumps in our throats. Our adrenalin glands began working. We saw the Ultimate. One by one, we rose and filled the courtroom with our voices, personalities, souls, dreams.

The reporters sat there, half of them crying, with twisted faces, and not moving a muscle.

Going to court every day had become a way of life for them and us—and in the end we were off to jail for five years and they were going home.

Each defendant felt a surge of heavenly energy and spirit that the life force provides women and men with in such moments.

*Schultz and Foran were forced to see us Naked.*

Dave began, voice quivering.

Tom said the system was destroying itself.

Rennie, "When I get out I'll move next to you, Foran, and turn your kids into Viet Cong."

Abbie's mouth became a sword and his humor had poison in it.

I paced around the room like a wild animal, and tried to give Julie a copy of my book with this inscription: "Dear Julie. You incited more riots than we ever could. You radicalized more young people than we ever could. You're the nation's top yippie."

Everyone had tears in their eyes.

The room was like a classic drama. Hardly anyone heard Julie then sentence us to five years. Marshals took us into the lock-up and the lock-up door shut for the last time on the Conspiracy Trial.

## Friday, July 10

Before 1967 things always happened first in California, then spread East by myth and media: first student demonstration (FSM), first anti-war demonstration (VDC), hippies, Haight-Ashbury. California, the place where all Amerikans go to start a new life, offered us the freedom and abandon and sunshine to start the movement.

People in Berkeley used to see themselves as the only national center of the movement. But energy had to spread and California lacked one thing: it lacked all the props for our theater.

Now everything happening everywhere.

Each area put its particular stamp mark on the spirit. San Francisco produced the Diggers and New York the Motherfuckers. The Weatherman came out of the steel and concrete and stubbornness of Midwestern cities. New York gave birth to the Yippies.

In 1969 the revolution broke out in the South and in March there were 10,000 freaks on the steps of Nashville, Tennessee, Capitol Building chanting FUCK YOU GEORGE WALLACE with a Southern twang.

We must create free communities, liberated areas, free cities, where young people can live together under our own rules and values for our own benefit. These youth ghettos will be the foundation of the revolution and they should exist in every city/town.

If successful, they will be painted in red in the map on the wall of the Pentagon and therefore might some day experience napalm and all-out bombing, as we have to consider adaptations, like the underground cities built by the Viet Cong. But that is a while off.

The first attempts at such community building—Haight-Ashbury and the Lower East Side—collapsed because of police presence, heroin, psychedelic capitalism and our inability to get our shit together.

Creating a community is tough in New York because our communities must be based on living communes, not individual apartments, and space is impossible to find in New York.

Our culture is redefining the family. To us friendship ties are greater than blood ties.

Blood may be thicker than water, but love is thicker than blood.

We learned a lot of things from our parents—foremost of which is DON'T GET MARRIED. No one gets married any more. For us our family is our sisters and brothers. Every friend is a "sister" and "brother." Living in small apartments by yourself cuts you off from others because real friends must live together. The strength of our movement is in friendship, and friends work and play together, and work out life's problems together.

The commune, not the private family, is the basic living unit in the revolution. We must break down the defenses and walls which we build against one another.

The Weatherman startled the movement with their bold declaration that monogamous relationships are counterrevolutionary because they are exclusive and based on dependency needs. Because we live in a sexist society every woman's goal in life is to find a man and become his emotional support and housekeeper.

Women's Liberation rose up against this system in 1969 and left in its wake thousands of broken relationships and destroyed male egos (including mine). The male-dominated movement was created out of Amerikan society and therefore accepted the bullshit advertising image of women in Amerika as sex objects who cook, fuck and keep their man happy.

For us this was a monumental contradiction because we believed in the liberation of black people, Vietnamese—but not women!

How many men in the movement have we met who have forced their wives to become submissive? Che's picture hangs on the wall, VICTORY FOR THE VIET CONG posters abound everywhere, but there is the "chick" forced to do all the cooking and cleaning and the men doing all the talking and the man defining reality and the woman feeling she has to look pretty. Movement men talked about women as pieces of ass just as bad as jocks do (well, almost).

Movement men objectify women.

And in movement organizations there were all the women in one room doing the typing and there were all the men in the other room sitting around the table like some fancy board of directors making all the decisions. No movement could survive based on such a contradiction. No movement can survive which suppresses the energy and potential of its people.

*Amerika has turned women into slaves.*

The fight of women is a liberation struggle, and it must take place within the revolution as well as against capitalism and imperialism. The organization of women into separate collectives saved women because only women can liberate themselves and this begins when they struggle against their oppression *as women* in Amerika and in the movement.

**HOUSEWIVES ARE POLITICAL PRISONERS.**

The Achilles Heel of Amerika is its suppression of women.

What would the business executives do if their wives revolted? What would happen to business if secretaries rose up against their oppression? Amerikan advertising is built around the domestication of the female kitchen slave. Young girls are faced with the horrendous models that Madison Avenue produces.

Women in the movement are putting forward their own model of liberation: women who speak, write, lead and fight.

Male supremacy is so deep in Amerika that it is unconscious.

*Do It!* had a lot of sexism in it but it took women and gay people to help me see that.

I was blind to it.

In *Do It!* the Pentagon and other forces of evil including Amerika itself were referred to as "she."

Revolutionaries were "he."

One sentence even proclaimed: "A new man was born at the Pentagon."

Implicit in the book is the image of yippie as male, as a "tough" revolutionary who can kick the shit out of pigs with one hand and fuck "chicks" at the same time.

On a deep level the yippie in *Do It!* is very macho, very Amerikan: competitive, ego-oriented, individualistic. Heterosexual sex is unconsciously accepted as the norm and *Do It!* made it insulting to say that Richard Daley and J. Edgar Hoover are in the back room making love.

Better for them if they are!

We male yippies have got to fight our honkyism. "I need a chick tonight—who should I call?" is the way too many male yippies rap to one another.

*Do It!* poured out of my Amerikan unconscious, shaped by a male chauvinist point of view: The yippie as Superman.

We are purging Amerika out of us and remaking ourselves into a healthy, loving humanity without a bloated ego or a domination-submission way of relating to each other.

The liberation of women will liberate men from their macho: fuck any woman I want to and beat the shit out of anybody who crosses me. I'm a man!

There's all kinds of macho. There's John Wayne-Green Beret macho. There's intellectual macho: fighting for intellectual positions competitively. The goal is not to discover insights, but to impress people, intellectual one-upmanship. Men debate intellectually and abstractly against other men and women to win approval and victory.

This kind of macho oppresses men because it keeps men in a competitive prison. Macho men like to be surrounded by people who are too weak to challenge them to go through changes.

Such macho can lead to a dangerous political adventurism. It is macho which keeps the US mired deep in the mud of Vietnam. There's a little jailhouse wisdom that says most men are in jail because of a woman. Men kill and fight each other for the possession of women. The women's liberation movement, unfortunately, tends to put men on a self-hate guilt trip. Fuck guilt. Guilt never freed anybody. Women and men together must work out personal and political alternatives to chauvinism.

"Women" alone will not make the revolution—all "people" will. Women must not dismiss men in the same way men used to dismiss women, and men must not hate themselves the way women used to hate themselves.

Together we will overcome our pasts, explode narrow sexual categories and definitions and reinforce each other's strengths.

We must create Communist record companies, Communist publishing houses, Communist distribution networks so that we can rescue ourselves from exploitation.

All great art today is revolutionary.

Controlling all our own art is our way to liberation and creating communities.

What if Dylan's profits went to financing revolution rather than Columbia Records?

If we got the profits of *Woodstock* rather than Warner Bros., we could

have used that bread to bail out of jail every black person held because she or he can't afford the ransom.

Our financial base lies in our way of life—which is our art. Woodstock proved to capitalists that we are a huge untapped "market," both of production and consumption of art.

We produce it and then consume it too, for a price.

Publishing this book with Harper & Row is a cop-out but there was no alternative. We have to create that alternative.

To do this we are going to have to produce Commie entrepreneurs, which may be a contradiction in terms.

Rock groups say they don't like to do political movement benefits 'cause the sound system is usually shitty. We gotta get our shit together! We are a New Nation and we must begin to govern ourselves. We must also police ourselves so the pigs can stay out of our communities.

**To be a revolutionary it is not enough to grow your hair long and smoke dope.**

**To be a revolutionary it is not enough to throw away your bras and stop shaving your legs.**

We rebel against meaningless work and the silly Protestant Ethic but that doesn't mean that all work is bad. Working *for them* is bad.

Work *for us*, work for yourself, is good.

Work is play.

Cleaning the streets, washing toilets, cooking, building is fun when you are doing it not for profit but for your sisters and brothers in the community, for your extended family, for the nation. Rebellion against Amerika is empty without building a healthy alternative.

Destruction of what needs to be destroyed requires construction of what needs to be constructed.

The New Nation needs skills. We need "businessmen" who don't make money for themselves but who make money *for the community*. Of course they won't be "businessmen"—they will be part of a new breed of people. When we get these organized activities set up we can then pressure every rock group, performer, artist to withdraw their talents from pig Amerika.

We saved the music business, the movie business, the book business. We have injected new energy and life into our enemy. This was necessary because we needed to use them to destroy them.

In lambasting Simon and Schuster for publishing my book, yippie William Buckley quoted Lenin: "When we hang the capitalists, they'll sell us the rope."

Purist politics is bullshit: Dylan reached and radicalized a generation. Purism is a disease.

The fact that Harper & Row gets rich off this book upsets me, but I'll deal with that later.

First things first. After our media revolutionizes millions, then those revolutionized people will create our own institutions and destroy Simon and Schuster, Random House, Harper & Row, CBS. Better to have Dylan in millions of homes than not, because he doesn't want to get his hands "dirty" cooperating with capitalism.

In a "cooperation" between us and capitalism, we win and they lose.

In my treaty with Simon and Schuster, publishers of *Do It!*, I won and they lost.

The yippies scandalize the movement by trying to reach the masses of young people through TV, circuses and comic books.

Elitism and mediocrity go hand in hand.

We never compromised. Our art was presented just as we made it. We are sure enough of our own identity not to feel compromised when it appears on national TV or through a capitalist book publisher.

Many book publishers hire a freak editor to keep them in touch with "youth" but that's just an illusion. Doubleday's "youth" editor got turned on by *Do It!* and got the editorial board to agree to publish the book. They had to check it with Nelson Doubleday. He flipped out.

"I won't publish Jerry Rubin!" he screamed, vetoing the deal.

One after another capitalist businessmen turned down *Do It!* The honest ones gave honest censorship reasons. The dishonest ones hid the political pressures behind bureaucratic, aesthetic reasons. You have to search to find the real political reasons in our capitalistic society.

Nothing is censorship, nothing is "political" even though we know *everything is political.* "Too hot." "We'd never do it." It wasn't because they couldn't make money, but because they were ideologically scared.

Finally Simon and Schuster and Ballantine accepted it.

S and S's long-haired token, Danny Moses, fought hard and they didn't yet have a token Commie writer.

I don't think they understood it but so what? They understood the reaction: a heavy, organized attack on them by the right wing. Letters poured in. Buckley and the Birchite *Human Events* attacked the book. Booksellers refused to stock it. Distributors rebelled. They received 500 right-wing letters a week and answered all of them.

Despite the fact that Simon and Schuster made lots of bread off *Do It!,* the political pressure was too great and they refused to publish *We Are Everywhere*. They made an original offer because the staff, especially my editor, Danny Moses, dug it. But when the pressure got down the president of the board of directors of the corporation suppressed the book: "Simon and Schuster will no longer publish Jerry Rubin."

He was smart: he was acting out of his own class interest.

Virtually every other publisher in Amerika refused to publish *We Are Everywhere*, and the pattern was the same: the staff and editors dug it and wanted to until the corporate presidents heard about it and said: NO!

Finally Harper & Row accepted. The goal of this book is to destroy Harper & Row.


We must create our own publishing communes and distribution networks because soon no book publisher will touch us and record and movie industries will get Agnewized as TV has been.

Hip capitalism is as great a threat to the youth culture as honky capitalism.

Capitalism is capitalism.

We should use the hip capitalists but we must realize that they have a stake in the money system and therefore are our enemies, not our friends.

Some hip capitalists can be turned on to living Communism. Other hip capitalists will have to be ripped off. A cold war now exists between hip capitalism and the revolutionary youth culture, but as things get hotter in this country, hip capitalists will have to choose between their money and their soul.

The hip capitalist reduces our culture to abstract objective goods and symbols. To defeat the hip capitalists, we are going to have to do what they do—but better.

Through collectives and the energy of the people, we must create a Communist economy within the belly of the beast to serve the people and put our values into practice as a daily lifestyle.

Madison Avenue will be burned to the ground.

The crime of the advertising industry against the humanity of women by reducing them to kitchen slaves and sex objects is a crime against the people and should be dealt with by the collective and violent wrath of angry revolutionary women and men.

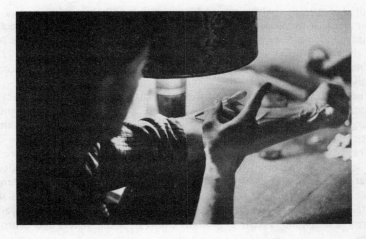

We have to create our own Communist islands within a capitalist sea, controlling our own art, setting up free stores, free food centers, free medical and dental clinics, free legal services, bail funds, crash pads, music co-ops, free garages, switchboards, housing collectives. The deterioration of our main streets like Telegraph Avenue, Haight-Ashbury, St. Marks Place, have to be dealt with.

We have to drive the heroin pushers out of our community. Heroin is one of the weapons used against black people and freaks. Grass and heroin are not the same. Grass does not lead to heroin.

*White milk leads to heroin.*

Pigs push heroin.

The heroin of Amerikan middle-class life and the heroin of the school system leads to young kids putting heroin in their veins.

Heroin is made a crime to give wardens and jail guards employment, pigs something to do and keep the public alarmed about "law and order."

**Christianity is addictive.**

Pot is not.

**Cigarettes are addictive.**

Pot is not.

Sisters and brothers have to take care of sisters and brothers who get trapped into heroin. Heroin is the government's most powerful counter-revolutionary agent, a form of germ warfare. Since they can't get us back into their system, they try to destroy us through heroin. We must create a revolutionary movement and community which will give people an alternative to despair and heroin.

## THE CHOICE IS REVOLUTION OR HEROIN.

All the colleges, universities and high schools will close permanently, or be taken over permanently by students. The ruling class of the schools will collapse under the weight of its own despotism. Some will send in the pigs to lock the buildings up. Others will let us take over the resources.

The campus anarchy after Cambodia and Kent State will be a permanent condition.

The liberation of energy from the conscripted labor of the educational system of Amerika will shake the planet. Out of this will come the new communities, Commie economic institutions, experimental societies that we must create to survive. Youth will become an army against Amerika.

The white nonstudent communities that have survived the best are those near university communities, like Berkeley and Madison. The stability of a university community gives the nonstudent community some permanence.

We nonstudent freaks already liberated from university prisons should create liberated nonstudent enclaves but should also work to subvert and destroy the school system that holds the rest of our sisters and brothers in chains.

I'm sitting in the back seat of this car, a 1969 Rambler, and I have to pinch myself to make sure I'm not going through a super hallucination.

My hands are double handcuffed and chained to my stomach and my legs are tightly shackled.

I'm chained to Art, a brawny bank robber who's on his way to Marian Penitentiary to spend the next 35 years of his life. On my right in the back seat is Duffy, a young black man who is serving a five-to-life sentence in San Quentin for armed robbery. We're driving through Wyoming, and it's beautiful. But our drivers, two federal marshals, won't let us out of the car to see the scenery.

Don, one of the marshals, keeps complaining how the FBI gets all the media credit when it's really the federal marshals who do all the work. He has a gun at his hip and keeps a close eye on Art while flicking the radio on and off and asking me question after question about "the revolution."

The other marshal, Percy, is the heavy silent type. He keeps sucking gum drops and holding his blackjack—just in case. Whenever you ask Percy a question, he'd reply, "Ask Don."

He's not supposed to talk to us.

We are moving from California to Chicago, a five-day journey. Every night at 5 P.M. we stop driving and the three prisoners are deposited at the nearest county jail for "safe keeping" overnight while the marshals go on to a motel.

At 6 A.M. the drive resumes again. I dig it. It's a nice way to spend jail time. I'm on my way to Chicago for the Conspiracy Trial. I ask Don why the government doesn't save money and just fly us there. "It's cheaper this way," he says, "and besides, some of your friends might hijack the plane to Cuba."

At lunch we stop at out-of-the-way truck stops. We've got a $1 minimum but we must eat with our handcuffs on. And when one of us has to go to the can we all gotta go 'cause we're chained together. That's so in case one tries to escape the others are chained to him.

Pretty tough trying to pull down your pants and shit with handcuffs and chains on.

We spent our nights at county jails in Reno, Salt Lake City, Cheyenne and Council Bluffs, Iowa.

Art told me what happened to him on a similar trip across the country two years earlier. He made a key out of a ballpoint pen and quietly unlocked his handcuffs.

Then, in a surprise move, he leaped out of his seat and over the head of the driver, grabbed his gun and held it at his head. "Now you'll take orders from me," Art said.

He ordered the marshals to drive him to a wooded area where he tied both marshals to a tree and drove away with their clothes, guns, money and car.

He was free for two years and made the FBI Top 10 but finally got caught in a shoot-out in his umpteenth bank robbery a few months earlier.

After the Conspiracy Trial we were in a rare position to create some revolutionary institutions. Liberal guilt money flowed in.

Finally we were in a position to get lots of bread for projects controlled by crazy motherfuckers. Even some of the Kennedy and McCarthy money was coming our way.

The Conspiracy was a billion-dollar project.

Rarely in history does the left discover such an oil well.

We could have made a killer movie and record about the trial, and the presence of any of us anywhere was worth $1,000 a crack at least.

Ronnie Davis, founder of the Mime Troupe, wanted to take us as a group around the world re-staging the trial in huge coliseums and sports arenas.

We were the new movie stars of the nation.

John Wayne was dead.

We were alive. Seven-stoned political revolutionaries were the hottest rock group in Amerika. The Justice Department had helped create its own revolutionary monster. We could have begun to create a national organization. We could have created a Conspiracy book publishing and record company.

But we learned something.

It is a lot harder to deal with success than failure.

We had thousands of dollars—what to do with it?

Could we become the people's bank?

How would we decide what to give money to? We couldn't, so we gave virtually all of our money and contracts to the Black Panthers, with some to Weatherman and the rest to the movements in Seattle and Santa Barbara.

Primarily there was just too much internal hassling. We could not find the people to work in the office or supervise projects. Each of us wanted some privacy after five months of going to court every day from 10 to 5. Hayden wanted The Conspiracy to die as soon as possible.

Abbie & I, fuck, we would have been in favor of producing Conspiracy tee shirts and rolling paper—we wanted to go the whole way!

We wanted to create ways in which the seven of us could take a back seat, decision-making be democratized and decentralized, and alliances be made with women's liberation groups since we were all men.

We felt it was outrageous for us to fold when the eighth Conspirator, Bobby Seale, still languished in captivity.

The Conspiracy died quietly: no movie, no play, no globe-trotting re-enacting tour by the defendants. It started with a bang! and went out barely with a whimper. All that incredible energy evaporated overnight. No ongoing work continues—only lawyers and appeals. All that is left are memories and the myth.

Maybe The Conspiracy was an unnatural, inorganic animal and could not continue as a model for young people because it contained too many diffuse elements? The Conspiracy had made its mark on History. Its day was over.

It would be back in the streets if the appeals court denied our appeals—a likely event.

For now History throws new faces and organizations into the battlefield. A vacuum is good because it contains unforeseen possibilities. The best thing about life is its unpredictability, the mystery.

Besides, despite it all, yippie was still bigger than The Conspiracy, more powerful, a bigger family.

It was easy, effortless, to kill The Conspiracy. We just closed the office.

*It was impossible to kill yippie.*

Just that taught us something.


Occasionally I'd be brainwashed by the prosecution and I'd want to call Bill and Lennie over and say: "Say, Schultz is right. We didn't want a permit for Lincoln Park. We made it as embarrassing as possible—threatening smoke-

ins, fucking immoral behavior—so we wouldn't get a permit. We wanted a violent confrontation so Amerika and the Democratic convention could be exposed as a police state.

"The Mob, shit, no ruling class in its right mind would allow thousands of people to march right to the amphitheater."

We won. That's why we're on trial, 'cause we won.

But can you be put in jail for what you *want*? We did apply formally for a permit. It was Daley and the police who drove us out of Lincoln Park and *they* aren't on trial. The police wanted a riot too. When they busted me they asked me: "Who won?" They saw it as a contest.

Yet, on the other hand, there was a part of me which really wanted a permit so we wouldn't get hurt. If we had gotten a permit early, we might have brought the promised 500,000 people to Chicago and that would have been another kind of victory over the pigs. So maybe my intent was pure and nonviolent. I know my head was not into killing pigs or dynamiting buildings then. We were accused only of calling people to come to Chicago, calling press conferences, opening offices, making speeches.

Put simply, our crime was the calling and organizing of a national demonstration in the same city as the Democratic convention at the same time.

I paid special interest whenever my name was mentioned although it was hard to *really believe* they were talking about *me*. I paid more attention when they were talking about the yippies.

I dug every word the judge said and I loved to stare him down. Many times I'd catch him staring at me. I'd then stick my tongue out at him. These are the great moments that will never appear in the printed record.

Julie got most incensed when we laughed. He always got the impression we were laughing at him. Once Julie said, "Will the record show the expression on that defendant's face." We wish the printed record could show the expression on Julie's face, the tone of his voice.

Facial expressions and voice tones are so much more important than the words anyway!

**IF OUR TRIAL HAD BEEN TELEVISED, THERE WOULD HAVE BEEN INSURRECTION IN THE STREETS AFTER ONE DAY.**

How could newspapers capture the contempt for us on Julie's pathetic, alcoholic face, the face that was getting even with us for all the wrongs done him all his life?

Julie was so outrageous that reporters and observers in the courtroom would daily sit with mouths open and breath stopped in total disbelief. Every new observer to the court would experience what amounted to a religious conversion seeing that madman on the throne. His capacity for sadism was endless. He did exactly what a judge should not do: he took everything personally.

Julius provoked most of the disruption in the courtroom by picking up the slightest voice, remark, or smile and saying, in front of the jury, "Let the record show that the defendant Davis smiled."

"I did not smile," said Rennie, prompting Dave to say, "It was me who smiled, Your Honor!" Then Abbie jumping up, "I smiled," then all of us smiling broadly.

First we were shocked. But the human body can only take so much shock until out of self-protection shock turns into a little laughter and smile. Gradually our shock turned to laughter and smiles at Julie's incredible tyranny. We smiled to keep our sanity.

After a while even oppression becomes funny.

Julie struck us as driven by such hate, so paranoid, that we felt at any moment he would cross the line and flip out. We gave him enough rope to hang himself. Over-escalation by the judge was our only hope 'cause the courtroom was so rigged.

Julie was our best ally in the courtroom cause he represented Reality.

Are we guilty because our behavior provokes Amerika to reveal its ugliness?

Honestly, we did very little in that courtroom.

Just being there was enough. Is it our long hair? Is it because we represent their own lost youth, lost dreams? Yippie has leveled a powerful psychological attack on the Amerikan ego. They don't like the fact that we are having a good time being alive.

To maintain their own lie—to themselves—they got to smash us. Amerika

must destroy us because we force it to see itself, and the truth is too horrible. We represent the impulses and instincts they deny in themselves. **Therefore they must kill us.**

Tim Leary, master manipulator of the images of the media, says that we should always smile whenever the press comes to photograph or film us! Even if they're dragging us off to jail. Smile! He's right. 'Cause they hate to know we're happy.

### Saturday, July 11

Here we were accused of violent crimes, fomenting revolution, and just look at us—we are gentle, loving people. The pigs who testified against us were all the same build—6 foot 2 inches, 230 pounds, and the way they carried their bodies said: "I'm a man. No hippie, nigger, gook or fag is gonna push me around." Their muscles and tough exterior remind them that they are men. And there we are—wasted on grass, small in stature, gentle in soul—violent only because something about us provokes them to violence.

That's why "dirty words" became such a huge issue in the trial. "Men"—*real men*—do not use such language before women. And so we had the spectacle of policemen on the stand all of a sudden bowing their heads like they're in church, getting sheepish looks on their faces and saying, "Your Honor, I can't say what the defendant then said because there are ladies present." Permission was then granted by the judge in the interest of Courtroom Truth, and the copper would say, "Your Honor, he said, 'Kill the fucking pigs! Kill the fucking pigs!' "

One witness, a lady cop, said my every other word in a speech in Lincoln Park was "fuck." Man, to them pigs every word out of our mouths is fuck or shit—or something they consider dirty! Everyone in the courtroom but us, the press and audience accepted this hypocrisy 'cause who would doubt that as soon as the pigs got out of the Federal Building and back to the other cops they didn't say, "Those fucking defendants, those cockroaches, they ought to get their asses whipped, they probably fuck each other."

We just don't talk the way they quoted us after taking solemn oaths on the Bible on the witness stand. They were putting *their* words in *our* mouths. They were saying what they would have said in the same situation if they were us. They were hearing the voices in their own heads.

On the witness stand the police are as immaculate as the Pope. It's part of the Christian tradition: speak decently in church (or on trial), before women, or in public, speak honestly in private. Amerika talks peace and practices war. Amerika loves blacks and destroys blacks. For us it is this dichotomy, this hypocrisy, that is the only obscenity.

But this honesty, our long hair (which makes men look like women—how disgusting), the dirty words out of our mouths makes the Amerikan Male unsure of his own masculinity. So it came to us as no surprise when, locked in our cages in Cook County Jail, we heard that Foran had called us all "fags" and said, "We are losing our kids to the freaking fag revolution."

Right on, Tom Foran!

Foran said he kept his sanity in the trial only by going every weekend to his son's basketball games—to see "real men in action."

We do not prove our humanity by our biceps. But we had the most courage in the courtroom. We were fearless. We had the courage of our convictions and were taking the consequences of our beliefs.

The Chicago *Tribune* had to rationalize this quality by writing an editorial saying as dedicated Commies we had now entered the martyrdom phase of

*Leila Khaled, guerrilla*

the revolution, taking long imprisonment and suffering to take the revolution to a higher stage. After all, Commies don't suffer 'cause they're not really human; the Viet Cong aren't human so they don't really die. That was pure bullshit. We laughed when we read it, but it also scared us too because it seemed to rationalize (to them) their putting us in jail for a long time.

We were scared but we were energized, motivated by the love of our sisters and brothers, by the example set by our comrades in Vietnam and black communities, by our feeling that we symbolized the Future and History. But we were not the *Tribune*'s martyrs. We bleed, suffer and cry like all human beings. Our courage under fear frightened the prosecution.

Our lack of their kind of "masculinity" filled them with contempt for us.

When we were sentenced for contempt we broke down and cried. Who can ever forget the sight of Bill Kunstler on his knees, crying and imploring, "Your Honor, take me now. You've destroyed everything I believe in," after marshals had attacked Michelle and Tasha Dellinger, Dave's daughters, while Dave was being jailed for contempt. I cried, too.

I cried at the horror and cruelty and viciousness that I had become a victim of. I cried at what I had *seen*. But we know that grown "men" do not cry. "Men" do not express their feelings, their hurt, in public. To Foran's

126

Catholic eyes we became sissies. But we were strong enough to cry. We were pure emotion.

It took an awful lot of repression NOT to cry at some moments in that trial.

Machines do not cry.

Human beings do.

Our cry was not a plea for mercy. When given an opportunity to speak before contempt sentences "for mitigation," with tears in our eyes and hurt and anger in our hearts, we leveled such an attack on the judicial system that the judge ordered the marshals to physically push us into our seats and shut us up.

Most of us aren't nonviolent. We will not shoot first because we are sickened at the sight of blood, but we will kill those who try to kill *us*—or our sisters and brothers.

None of the defendants was over six feet. Our hair is more distinctive than our muscles. One look at us could tell that we were ex-intellectuals, not jocks. Yet this motley, tiny, pacifistic-looking group had been accused of terrorizing a city, of organizing a riot and conspiring to overthrow the government. We looked like a rock band, not a football team. We represent those who are

accused of being chicken to go over there and defend our country—but who, strangely enough, are brave enough to take on individually the most powerful and arrogant government in the history of the world right here in its own backyard.

We are redefining what it means to be a "man," a "woman" and a "human being" in Amerika in practice, and cleansing ourselves from the phony sick notions we learned at home, school, in the media.

Even though all the drama and evidence concerned the events of August, 1968, when we were really innocent, the trial had a vicious edge of The Future in it. The crimes we were accused of doing we had done in mind only.

In August, 1968, sabotage and bombings and fighting back against cops had really not taken place yet among white youths. August, 1968, was the last of the nonviolent illusions. The bloody attack on us played a role in ending those illusions. No defendant was accused of any violent, physical act. All the evidence against us was words. Words, words, words.

Letters of the alphabet. Sounds. Noises. Voices. Sentences. Those were our crimes. Paragraphs.

There were some funny moments. My "tail" testified that one morning in disgust I threw my sweater at him. The room held in suspense at the revelation of this vicious act. Kunstler grit his teeth, gulped and asked solemnly, "I take it you were not seriously injured by the sweater?"

From November on—for nine months—me, Abbie, Tom, Rennie, Dave and many other women and men, usually at odds, with Tom and Rennie wishing yippie would disappear as a bad apolitical nightmare and us seeing the Mob as a relic of the nineteenth century—pushed the Chicago demonstration like motherfuckers to the opposition of most of the movement. People were vehemently for or against. Such hoopla promotion is necessary for a big national demonstration.

Before the demonstration began it was clear to the FBI that *we* would be the ones to be indicted.

Undercover pigs were then placed on us to find *something, anything,* illegal to build up their case.

I remember after speaking with Bobby Seale Tuesday night in Lincoln Park in maybe my most fire-eating speech, my so-called bodyguard Bob Pierson dug it the most. He kept patting me on the back and saying, "Great speech, Jerry! Fuck, man, that was great!" He dug it more than anyone else. I thought to myself, "Well at least I'm reaching the workers." Little did I know he was a Chicago policeman!

Tony Lukas of the *New York Times,* Jason Epstein of Random House et al., couldn't believe we were guilty. I jokingly kept telling them that we were—but they wouldn't hear me, they refused to listen, they kept saying, "Oh no you're not." You see, these liberals could not defend us *if we were guilty*. We had to be innocent victims of a First Amendment violation. We wanted our friends to defend us because we *were* guilty.

The FBI understands what is going on better than the liberals. But the liberals gotta understand that the FBI is the enemy—no matter what we do.

It is irrelevant whether we are innocent or guilty. We are better revolutionaries if we are guilty. Our lawyers, Lennie and Bill, agreed with the liberal observers, but they had to. Believing in your defendant's innocence is an occupational hazard. To be good actors—and above all else a lawyer is a good actor or actress—they had to believe their lines. A lawyer believes to the end his client's innocence.

In fact, Lennie and Bill never asked us if we were guilty or innocent. They just set out to tear apart their case—and put on our best defense. Good criminal lawyers. It's funny—the prosecution may have been right mythically but they were wrong on virtually all the details.

Their versions were an undercover's fantasy of what went on since most of their evidence came from undercover agents. It was ridiculous! I could have prosecuted us better than they did. They missed the best points. Virtually everything they said I did I didn't do, and what I did do they missed. I'm sure that went for the other defendants too.

What happened between the crime and the trial? The war intensified. Nixon became President. Eldridge was forced out of the country. Woodstock fulfilled the dream the yippies had for Chicago—500,000 people going apeshit in Chicago. The Weatherman took the struggle to higher levels. People's Park saw demonstrators shot for the first time in the streets. Bobby Seale jailed on a bogus beef—possibly for the rest of his life. John Sinclair, White Panther, jailed for 10 years for one joint and Pun forced underground on a score of beefs. During the trial Fred Hampton assassinated in the middle of his sleep in bed. Mylai revelations.

### Sunday, July 12

In another respect the trial foreshadowed Tomorrow: The government admitted in open court that it had tapped our phones for years, and that it had the legal right to do so. Fuck those who object. If the Justice Department considered us dangerous to national security, they could tap our phones, without a court order. Liberals objected, but soon accepted it. Undercover agents infiltrated our organizations, observing meetings, office work, ordinary political activity—and in some cases initiated the very illegal activity they accused us of. The government unashamedly chose Julius Hoffman as "Impartial Judge" of our trial. No more pretenses at liberalism or fairness.

The FBI ran our trial.

Still the government had to obey some legal hang-ups. They had to have a trial and give us the *illusion* of a *jury trial*. They had to let us put on a defense even though when our defense got too effective—like calling the ex-Attorney General to the stand on our behalf, Ramsey Clark—they kept him from eyesight of the jury and kicked him off the witness stand. They didn't want the jury to know that we had LBJ's Attorney General on our side .

They probably bugged the jury room and jurors' hotel rooms so they knew what was going on there too. I mean, wouldn't you if you were the government?

Who polices you? No one.

You're playing for keeps. Fairness means nothing when "national security" is at stake. Who would know? Or better still, you infiltrate the jury. You put your FBI or CIA person on the jury.

We believe to this day that one of the jurors, Kay Richards, who is twenty-three years old, was a police agent. She was the only young juror so she'd be the least suspect. She wrote in her exclusive post-trial *Sun-Times* series that she used to deliberately smile at the defendants, wink at us, react favorably to our evidence to give *us* the impression that she was on our side and we were getting a fair trial even though all along she believed that we were completely guilty. She fooled us too. I remember the day of jury selection. One thousand people filled the special courtroom. It looked like a meeting of the Birch Society. We gasped, BAD VIBES—all! The young faces in the room stood out like gold jewels. Kay sat right next to our table and flirted with us. She smiled. She cooed. She yipped.

We were so taken in by Kay's age and smiles that we used to tell our witnesses to talk directly to her, ignoring the other jurors, who were all twice her age.

During the whole trial we did not know that Kay was engaged to marry a high-ranking official in the Cook County Sherrif's department. They got married after the trial.

All the jurors say no guilty verdict would have been achieved without Kay's psychological games. She first gave the other jurors the impression she was for acquittal, then changed her mind dramatically to conviction on both counts, then used her age as a weapon to convince the older jurors to compromise and find us guilty on one five-year charge.

She worked as a negotiator bringing the two factions of the jury—one for conviction, one for acquittal—into a bullshit compromise that no one believed in.

Immediately after the jury delivered its verdict Kay drove straight to a hotel room where she dictated her story to a newspaper for a load of bread.

*Don't trust anyone under thirty.*


We yippies have to be careful about becoming age chauvinists. Age is in your head, not your body.

Repression used to be fun. It ain't any more. Too many friends and lovers have been sentenced to prison for too many years. Too many friends and lovers have been driven into exile. Too many are underground.

In the past 48 months almost all of my close friends have been taken away by the state. Repression has become a personal thing, attacking our lives. For me the revolution now means freeing Pun, John, Sharon, Robin, Bobby, Sam and bringing Bernardine, Jeff, Bill and Jane—to name just a few—back into our living rooms.

We no longer have a choice whether or not to be a revolutionary and enemy of the state. The revolution means our friends, and we want our friends alive and free.


The revolution has become personal—and serious for young whites. Revolution means death or life. Revolution is also having a great time being alive—a constant up trip.

If that sounds confused, it's because I can't decide whether we are victims fighting fascism or aggressors against imperialism. I still don't know whether we were victims or aggressors in the courtroom in Chicago. I guess, both. Revolution is self-defense and revolution is joyous attack.

In the final analysis what happens is both sides, prosecution and defense, put on a play and create a myth for the jury. Two versions of history. Two theatrical performances. The jury then goes into the jury room and decides what play feels more *real* to them.

If we lose, we go to jail.

The prosecution has all the advantages because *we* are on trial, *we* are the accused, they make the charges and we answer their charges.

### Monday, July 13

What happens when eight Agnewized right-wingers and four anti-war liberals go behind locked doors to decide the fate of seven revolutionaries?

Mrs. Baldwin versus Mrs. Wallace.

Somehow the soul, the future, of Adult Amerika, Middle Amerika, was going to be symbolized by that confrontation. Can the liberals stem the right-wing tide of fascist Amerika?

Can they hold out? Or is it true that the liberals are chickenshit of losing what they have too and would rather compromise with Agnew than side with us? In a symbolic sense, our jury would decide that question of Amerika and its soul.

Are we, the youth, without commitment to this system, really alone? If the liberals are not brave enough to hold off the right wing in the corridors of power, are we forced to change Amerika in the streets?

The liberals will have to free Bobby Seale and Angela Davis nonviolently or we, the youth, black and white, will have to free them violently.

If the liberals want to avoid a violent revolution in the streets, they must destroy the vicious state violence of the US nonviolently.

Maybe the liberals believe in this system more than they oppose its crimes? If so, we are really up shit's creek.

We are alone.

These thoughts dangled somewhere in my unconscious as the jury went out and I thought of Mrs. Baldwin and Mrs. Wallace and Eugene McCarthy and Spiro Agnew.

*(l. to r.): Lee, John, Dave, Jerry, Rennie, Tom, Abbie*

We were in jail—and the jury was deliberating. There seemed something very logical about that. Julie was going to put us away with or without the help of the jury. We were locked up in the hole to quarantine us from the rest of the prisoners.

Abbie was the most down 'cause he had been sentenced to only eight months for contempt and nobody could understand that. Abbie was planning to jump up next time in court and demand justice. He was just down, quiet, moody.

The jury was out—what the fuck did it matter? The jury deliberations were pure anticlimax. Who would have thought that the jury would become so irrelevant?

I felt an intense hatred and bitterness. Already in jail! Julius out-does Julius! What chutzpah! What nerve! What did it matter what we did in the courtroom—here was Hayden with more time than Abbie. I felt shell-shocked, like a ton of bricks had fallen on my head and left me overwhelmed and dizzy. I thought Julie would shock us at the end but this was too much—beyond our wildest nightmares.

On our tier were black prisoners who had been locked up by themselves for months, fed under the jail door by guards they never saw, slop they couldn't eat, with no contact with anything human. Through the day and night they talked to themselves—steady, mad, desperate, insane sounds.

*The terror of the jail matched the terror of the courtroom.*

Hayden and I were locked up together in one tiny cell, he on the bottom bunk, me on the top, and for the first time I felt so beautifully close to him. How petty were our disputes when faced with such brutality.

"You guys the Conspiracy 7?" one black guy asked. "Yeh!" we answered. "Hey, you guys really gave it to the court! You really did it! We're with you! It's about time someone got those motherfuckers!" We were heroes in jail, heroes to the black prisoners decimated by thousands of Julius Hoffmans, large and small.

The jury was out but who the hell gave a damn? All I remembered was Nancy crying, head in her hands, as two marshals led me screaming "Sadist! Sadist!" out of the courtroom and into the lock-up. Hayden began writing an analysis of the contempt. He felt the press had badly hurt us by playing up disruption in the courtroom beyond what actually took place, and therefore enabled Julie to really give it to us. Abbie called the warden a pig and was put in a cell by himself.

Maybe we should go on a hunger strike? That would be easy. The food was dogshit. Tom was against it. "What for?" he asked. "What would it prove? It'd only hurt ourselves. We have to eat."

The controversies of the courtroom continued into the jail but by now who cared? Strangely I felt closer to Tom at that moment than Abbie 'cause Tom and I got so much contempt and Abbie so little. I didn't blame Abbie—it wasn't his fault—but we weren't in the same position at that moment so our heads weren't in the same place. The guards came by and we asked why we were locked in the hole and couldn't get out of our small cells to walk. He didn't know. He didn't make the decision—he was just carrying out orders, doing his job. Our questions irritated him. "What do you think this is, a hotel? This isn't the Hilton," he said, sneering and walking away.

The rat. The lousy shit-faced rat. Very funny. "This isn't the Hilton." "This isn't the Hilton." What kind of a sick human being can be a jail guard and say that to a human being locked up? Time passed. Morning to afternoon to night. The screaming continued. Oh, if middle-class Amerika could hear these screams!

Kunstler got more contempt than all of us. He even surpassed Bobby Seale. Surely Amerika is not going to stand for that! A lawyer getting four years for defending his clients with all his heart in court! Bill's effect on the law schools was incredible. The name "Kunstler" stood for something. A new myth of what a lawyer could be like. A lawyer was a criminal too. A lawyer fought an unjust system. No more lawyers on their knees before corrupt judges. Lawyers could be revolutionaries too. Lawyers go to jail too. Lawyers are fighters. Lawyers battle corrupt judges.

Whenever we were acting up Julie would look at Bill or Lennie, saying, "Well, what are you going to do?" Like they were supposed to be our parents or something, disciplining their kids. Lawyers, as officers of the court, are supposed to keep their clients in line. Julie gave Bill four years and Lennie two because he was personally pissed off at their love for us and disrespect for him—but also to deter other lawyers who might also defend clients like us. But like most repression, it backfired.

Early in the trial I said to Bill, "Bill, you gotta become a yippie. You gotta grow your hair long and live with us in a commune. When the trial is over you call a big press conference and announce that the court system is so corrupt that you are going to resign as a lawyer. There is no justice in the courts. You say you're becoming a yippie." Bill's eyes twinkled and he embraced and

kissed me. Bill is always embracing someone.

"No," he said. "You're going too far." But what I suggested took place. After the trial Bill became the hottest speaker on the campuses. He was now accused of being an inciter to riot himself, no longer just an uptown lawyer.

It would be a tragic comment on Amerikan middle-class morality if the mass of lawyers deserted him and only the fifteen-year-olds were left to defend him.

But they want to disbar Bill because he is a threat to their *club*. Funny thing about it, Bill has some faith in the system. He voted for Humphrey in 1968 fearing a Nixon victory. When he told me that in court one day I nearly fell out of my chair. "Bill, how could you?"

He believed we'd get a hung jury. He was sincerely shocked at Julius Hoffman and made every motion believing that any moment Julie would become a human being. Bill believes in the court system as one of the last hopes for freedom in Amerika today. Sentencing Kunstler and Weinglass to contempt demonstrated the seriousness of Julius's pathology.

Lennie was a tireless driving worker who knew the case upside down and who did most of the tough evidence work in the courtroom. The media did not feature or symbolize Lennie but he was the unsung hero of the trial. And none of us will ever forget Lennie's summation. He held the courtroom's breath as he battered the facts for five and a half hours and painted us as human beings. After Lennie finished, I was sure the jury would stand up and put on New Nation buttons.

"Why treat people like dogs?" I asked one jail guard.
*"If I treated you like I treat my dog, you'd be treated pretty damn well,"* *he replied.*
Amerika treats its pets better than it treats its minority groups.

Wednesday morning: The jury had been out five days. A hung jury seemed certain. We rooted for the jury like they were a ball team. We turned on the radio and heard that we were being brought in from the jail to hear a report from the jury. We got worried. Oh-oh. What could this be? Then we thought, this is probably on our motion to bring the jury in for a progress report. Or maybe the jury is coming in to report that it is completely and impossibly deadlocked? Yippie!
Five and a half months were coming to a dramatic end.
Guards came up to our tier and soon we were handcuffed and in the paddywagon on our way to the Federal Building—with one pig car in front of the wagon and a second behind, eight marshals on us with drawn shotguns. Wouldn't it be awful if some of us were found innocent and some guilty?
One theory was that the yippies would be found guilty because we most symbolized the jurors' fear as parents, attacking middle-class society with our hair and dirty words.
Rennie was particularly worried 'cause he thought he was likely to get off. He looked like the guy next door and he was brilliant and convincing on the witness stand. Foran later called it the toughest cross-examination he'd ever had.
They had the least evidence on Dave—but his age made him most likely to be found guilty.
The five of us felt ourselves to be equally guilty or innocent.
To get off would be the worst. It'd be the most painful. We hoped it was all or nothing. We arrived in the basement of the building and soon the handcuffs were off and we were on the elevator and in the courtroom where a strange ominousness hung in the empty room. Foran and Schultz sat there—quietly—did they know something? Julie entered and then his bailiff said, "Your Honor, the jury has reached a verdict."
The roof dropped. My stomach dropped. Tears welled in my eyes. I felt my head shaking. No, it can't be true. We looked at each other with the downest faces in the world. Our bodies raged with fury. A decision—it couldn't be good.
Schultz demanded that the courtroom be cleared.
Anita and Nancy and John Froines's mother-in-law sat in the courtroom. Marshals moved after them. Anita became a beautiful witch—she rose,

pointed a finger at Julie and shouted: "We'll dance on your grave, Julie!"

Nancy shouted, "There'll be demonstrations all over the country this week!" and all were pushed out of the courtroom.

Then the jury door opened. In walked the jury. One look at them and we knew what happened. Mrs. Baldwin's head was bowed and tears were falling down her face and she looked like she had just received tragic news. She was the picture of the pained sympathetic liberal. I stared at Mrs. Baldwin and just shook my head. I knew I would never see her again. I wanted her to never forget the hatred, fury, despair and disappointment in my face.

The rest of the jurors wore the satisfied faces of executioners. The Jewish woman in the back row seemed very sad. Kay Richards no longer winked at us. Mrs. Wallace had carried the day. The bailiff read the verdict.

Froines was cut loose. He began bawling.

Weiner found not guilty.

That was right—they never should have been indicted in the first place. Each of the five were found not guilty of conspiracy but guilty individually of crossing state lines to riot. I was too disappointed to be angry.

We asked for a roll call of the jury and each juror affirmed the verdict. I kept shaking my head. All of us were unbelievably shocked. The jury got up and left the courtroom for the last time, heading home. We got up and went into the lock-up, back to our new home, Cook County Jail. The trial was over.

As the jury bus drove out of the Federal Building for the last time hundreds of young people surrounded the bus, shouting "Pigs!" and throwing paper, rocks and stones at it. The jurors deserved it.

Who do I blame most? Julius Hoffman—no, he is a fossil and doesn't even know better. The hangwomen on the jury—no, they were pigs from start to finish and nothing could have changed their minds. I blame Mrs. Baldwin.

I blame the sympathetic liberal who understood what was at stake and could have just sat in the corner through all the deliberations and shaken her head no. In the end we found out there were three other women like Mrs. Baldwin who thought that we were not guilty but who *compromised*.

Compromise is a dirty word.

Liberals compromise.

Revolutionaries stand up for morality.

Compromise! Bullshit! You cannot compromise morality, life or death, guilt or innocence, freedom or imprisonment.

We have more to fear from liberals like Mrs. Baldwin who compromise with the right wing than we do from the right wing itself.

**We are all alone.**

We have only each other.

Sell-out and abstract intellectual middle-of-the-road liberals are the final hangmen and women of Western culture.

The pressure was too great. They did not want to be the ones responsible for defeating the federal government.

**You can trust a liberal to be a liberal.**

They voted in the end with the system and against justice.

Since there was no justice in the courts, they forced us into the streets.

They helped the FBI and Julius to put us away. They, of course, satisfy their consciences by believing that the case will be overturned on appeal by a higher court.

That smug satisfaction enables them to go to sleep at night knowing that they have failed their children and tomorrow's children.

*Someone else will do it.* But the same paralysis that overcame them will overcome the higher judges.

Ours is a political case.

Some very powerful people want us put away and the case blessed as a testament to Amerika.

Prince Crazy, George Demmerle, the FBI rat who for two years flipped through New York's streets as the craziest yippie of them all, says what he learned most from Abbie and Jerry was costumes. He wore the craziest clothes so no one suspected him of being a pig underneath. Amerikans respect costumes and uniforms.

For a while we thought the pigs wouldn't grow their hair long or wear our costumes, but George showed us we were wrong about that. Beware the wolf-pig in yippie-sheep's clothes! We must be sure not to take our own symbols too seriously.

All revolutionaries have long hair, but not all longhairs are revolutionaries.

All revolutionaries smoke pot but not all pot smokers are revolutionaries.

George used to always smoke a lot too. He dug pot. Marijuana is not an automatic revolutionary magic drug: there is no such thing as revolution through chemistry.

We yippies are great actors and actresses—put-ons—so we can easily be fooled by another great actor, put-on. The easiest person to put on is another put-on.

Pot's effect depends on the context. Pot usually brings your dreams and

fears and soul to the surface, which is revolutionary because the more people who ask "Who am I?" and examine their life, the more revolutionaries we have.

We are fighting the machine society and the machine man and machine woman. Pot is an anti-machine drug. Pot brings along with it the pot culture, which is anti-government and anarchic.

Pot is an honesty drug.

A truth serum.

An educational prop to discover your own soul. The fact that GI's and young business people and fraternity boys and sorority girls and some pigs and hip intellectuals smoke pot is a good thing. It weakens, in general, their commitment to law and order and defense of the military-industrial state and their anality but it also shows that pot does not make miracles.

The hippie honeymoon is over.

All hippies are enemies of the state. Since we are enemies, the alcoholic-money-nicotine-bombs-drug culture declares our religious sacraments illegal.

*Making pot illegal is like telling Jews that matzoh is now illegal.*

We are a new religion and they declare our sacred sacraments a crime.

Going after the sellers and letting the smokers off is a cop-out, a trick. That's like going after the inciters to riot but letting the rioters off. It is an attempt to divide our culture and buy some of us off. We must defend our grass pushers ferociously because, as Leary says, they are the ministers of our religion. While protecting them we must turn them on to economic freedom, Communism, making drugs free and doing it only for cost.

We gotta take all the personal profits out of selling pot. Charging money for grass is a hypocritical act—paying for dope is a downer. Pot should be free. If there are any profits, all the profits should go back into the freak community for the growth and development of the nation.

Pot profits should go to a national pot bail fund. All drug profits should go to free food programs, health centers, underground papers, guns, public celebrations, bombs, paying rent of communal houses so our sisters and brothers can live for free and not be forced to sell themselves in slavery to Amerikan society.


**Tuesday, July 14**


Pig Amerika operates on the deterrent notion of crime. Punishment will stop the crime.

In Berkeley sometime around 1967 the pigs stopped the misdemeanor honeymoon and began arresting anyone *caught* in a demonstration for a felony. It was a way of telling us: You people are criminals and will be treated as such.

The militancy of the movement has grown proportionately with the increased repression of the state. The more repression, the more militancy.

The FBI goes apeshit when it comes to a campus to find out who bombed the ROTC building and finds out no one will help them, not even the liberals, with information even though *everyone knows*.

Money can't buy us because we are not in this for the money.

Political turncoats are rare. Bob Pierson, Demmerle, Travelin' Tom, Larry Grathwohl and Steve Weiner were pigs who became hippies. Hippies do not become pigs. The solidarity on a campus is a beauty to behold. It began when pigs found demonstrators attacking them to free captured demonstrators.

A few scared freaks busted for dope have cooperated with the narcs to lay a trap for someone else but they can never live with themselves after doing it. We are a new culture, community, nation. We are a huge threat because we are not a political party like the Communist Party—we are a new culture. Repression has just forced us to escalate our tactics.

The movement moved to sabotage when our peaceful demonstrations and communities were violently attacked by the police. Chicago 1968 created the moral conditions for widespread sabotage. The entire community supported it because we all experienced the reality of police and state violence. Every major attack on us creates the moral conditions for more aggression on our part.

The Weatherman came onto the scene as far-out, crazy, flipped-out vanguard violence-loving people in October, 1969—but six months later, after the brutality of the Chicago Conspiracy Trial, the invasion of Cambodia, the murders at Kent State and Jackson, the legal assassination of Fred Hampton, virtually every campus in the country began using Weatherman tactics and Weatherman—without using the name or even being aware of it—began ap-

pearing everywhere. Weatherman became a typical response to state violence.

When it first appeared Weatherman was masochistic in its adaptation of Viet Cong tactics to the USA. By the time last spring rolled around, Weatherman tactics were a typical human reaction to an organic situation and liberal pacifism became a masochistic trip.

Cambodia and Kent State revolutionized as many people as the events of Chicago August '68. The death of the Kent State 4 will not result in young people no longer demonstrating. It means that revolutionaries are forced to shoot too.

The kids coming up will be more far-out than my generation. They do not share our repressed upbringing of "Free" Amerika facing Soviet Communism—ideas drummed into our heads as kids. We had to liberate ourselves from the hang-ups of Cold War fifties propaganda. We had to create something out of nothing. We even felt somewhat guilty demonstrating—we had to have long meetings and issue long leaflets and make all kinds of demands and give the deans and LBJ one more chance and say we wish we didn't have to do this—but.

The generations growing up today are born with Vietnam and pigs attacking black people and Kent State murders and White House hypocrisy as primary experiences from birth so where will they be at? Will they go through our steps? Teach-ins to marches to street fighting to sabotage? They are going to be *something else*.

The youth of the seventies will be Viet Cong and they will lead us.

But the yippies show that physical age is irrelevent.

Everyone thinks we're fifteen years old! During the trial a young kid, family friend of the Forans', came to the scene. I stopped him in the hall and

asked him what side the students in his Catholic high school were on. "A lot on your side," he said. "You know, 'cause you're young, and they're young, and you're on trial."

I went back into the courtroom and told that to Abbie. He laughed. "We're not young," he said. "Schultz is younger than we are."

*I had forgotten.* Abbie was right. We're both over thirty. Our prosecutor was a few years younger than us. In fact, Abbie is the father of two kids who came to the trial and ran up to him yelling, *"Daddy!"*

But our image is young kindergarten kids and it just shows that you can be a kid all your life.

Kids find out that we are over thirty and they discover something very important: you can be that old and still have so much fun! We believe in permanent childhood and we're showing kids that getting "old" doesn't mean becoming anxious and miserable and fear-ridden and cynical and sad and tired like their parents.

The courtroom is a religious institution like a church and standing up for the judge is important to get everyone into the Lie. If you were slow in rising, the marshal stared at you ferociously and held his gavel suspended in mid-air, then shouted, "Stand up, Mr. Davis!" and the entire courtroom—jury, marshals, judge, press—held its breath until you rose.

If a reporter or spectator didn't rise, he or she would be summarily kicked

out of the courtroom and never be permitted to return. For five and a half months every single reporter and spectator rose. We didn't rise only at key moments in the trial, and in the end we received one day in Cook County Jail for every time we didn't rise.

I wish we didn't rise during the whole fucking trial. We shouldn't stand up for judges or salute the flag or pay our income taxes or rent, or drop quarters and dimes in the toll meters on expressways across Amerika.

Those kinds of conditioned reactions are the stuff of which fascism is made.

Obedience to the state is a bad habit.

We must smash all the authority figures of the society. Destroy the magic aura behind power and you begin to destroy power. That's what is so great about calling policemen "pigs."

You desanctify a law by breaking it. Acceptance of a law means the law is powerful. The purpose of a law is to get *you* to police *yourself*. We must defy their rules and procedures—or they will get accepted.

We should smoke pot everywhere, especially in public streets. Mass smoke-ins are far out. Smoke in restaurants and especially at movie theaters. Smoking grass in movies is really outasight! Watch the people right around you sniff away and then happily discover what it is.

Smoke pot in the Student Unions and libraries of your local college. The campuses are our sanctuaries and battlegrounds. We go there to get in from out of the cold.

If you happen to accidentally recognize a fugitive at a movie theater or rock festival, don't freak out. Stay calm. Quietly go up to the person and empty out all your pockets and give all your belongings to him or her, especially money, food, vitamin C, credit cards, identification, checkbook, pot, driver's license, social security card.

Give the fugitive your beads, headband, the shirt off your back and then a big hug and kiss.

**Helping and hiding a fugitive is one of the best acts of a human being.**

The youth revolt means that our generation is creating its own mythology. Spiro Agnew can scream all he wants, but we don't respect him. We respect the Viet Cong and we consider the Amerikan soldier to be an outside invader, a mercenary killer.

"Thinking for yourself" means creating your own magic.

The true achievement of our trial—why we won and the government lost—is that we broke the magic of the courtroom. The spell is over. "Judge" is now a dirty five-letter word. A lot of middle-class people are now free enough from their automatic respect for courts to feel the injustice of the poor.

Smashing that magic is as important as the blowing up of 500 pig buildings through violence.

Symbolic victories are more important than physical victories.

The best sabotage is sabotage that destroys the society's magic and creates a new mythology. Sabotage and violence that is indiscriminate reflects a macho complex.

The true revolutionary strikes out at the symbol which oppresses the people, so the people can cheer the sabotage. It is important that the Conspiracy Trial *preceded* the bombing of the courthouse where Rap Brown was to be lynched.

The Conspiracy Trial so exposed the court system that when Rap Brown disappeared rather than stand trial lots of young people identified with Rap and were willing to help him. The Conspiracy Trial so exposed the judicial system that today millions of young people will hide and protect fugitives.

Sabotage which is not mythic and consistent with the feelings and passions of the people will be isolated. The more symbolic, the more people can *participate* in the act. Young people now feel that an underground is necessary because the pigs and courts and jails are barbaric murderous institutions and we must protect our own.

Lennie and Bill grew their hair long but kept their white shirts and ties on so that the jury and their contemporaries would at least still listen to them.

A lawyer without a suit and tie would be considered a babbling idiot.

Our defense table looked like a grassy field after a be-in. The remains of a hedonistic day were all around, from candy wrappers to wigs and jellybeans and books and letters. But nothing was out of place on the prosecution side. All orderly and neat. Neat piles and folders.

Death versus Life, Order versus Energy.

We even put our feet on the table. Mrs. Peterson, juror, told the press after the trial, "They had no respect for other peoples' property." We'd doze off and the marshal would, upon prodding by Julie, come by and wake us up. We'd slump in the chair to get comfortable and the marshal would come by to tell us to "sit up straight."

Five minutes later we'd be back slumping again. Keep those marshals earning their pay! It was like being in grade school again.

Julie kept his eye on us—like your homeroom teacher.

It would all get very absurd—but a lot of fun. We'd shout out a comment and be told to shut up by the head marshal. "But I was talking with my lawyer," you'd say. Shouting out is illegal but talking to your lawyer is okay. What if you talk loud enough to your lawyer so the whole courtroom can hear it?

One night we got stoned and the battle of psychological war versus Julie and the courtroom hit a new high. Wouldn't you love to see the expression on Julie's face if Abbie and Jerry walked into the courtroom wearing judge's robes! Wow! We both fell on the floor laughing so hard our insides hurt!

He might have heart failure right then and there.

Defendants wearing robes too—it would steal his show! He couldn't ignore it. The robes mean too much to him.

The jury couldn't ignore it.

But what could Julie do? It wasn't illegal. How could wearing judge's robes be considered contempt? That wouldn't be fair. Julie would stare at us all day. He'd never be able to get his eyes off us.

We zoomed over to a costume shop and got outfitted, laughing all the way. We just kept imagining that first expression on Julie's face!

We wore our winter coats into the courtroom so that marshals wouldn't stop us, then stripped them off and revealed to the full courtroom our flowing sacred robes. Julie's jaw dropped and his face reddened and his eyes glared and he froze.

With his eyes stonily fixed on our smiling, joyous bodies he stated: "Let the record show that the defendants Hoffman and Rubin entered the courtroom at 10:23 wearing collegiate robes."

"Judge's robes, Your Honor," I said. Muffled laughter filled the courtroom. Mrs. Baldwin twisted her face to conceal a laugh. Kay turned her head to hide her laugh. The press and spectators were in stitches. Julie didn't think it was funny.

"Okay," he said, "judge's robes."

"Black robes of death," someone uttered from the defense table.

Exasperated, Julie turned his death stare to Kunstler. "Is this another one of your bright ideas, Mr. Kunstler?"

Bill, suppressing a king-size belly laugh, said, "No, Your Honor, I'm sorry, I can't take credit for this one."

*A few minutes later Abbie took off his judge's robes and underneath he wore the blue and white shirt of a Chicago policeman.*

A moment of absolute truth descended over the courtroom.

We each got six days in jail for contempt of court for that act of theater.

Meeting blacks and Mexicans and Puerto Ricans in jail I find that I am indeed a member of a new *race*. I am not a "white man." I am a "hippie." "Are you a hippie?" I'm asked. I nod. A brother-to-brother handshake. I am accepted as an equal. Blacks know that hippies are black too.

It's a paradox but the worst days in jail are visiting days and the toughest moments mail call and the hardest time to do is on weekends.

Today is my birthday and I'm noncelebrating it in Cook County Jail.

I hope no one knows because it would be too sad. Weekends are the worst 'cause somewhere deep in your mind you are thinking of what you might be doing if you weren't there.

A black guy who just served 10 years for murder and now is back on a robbery beef, and who has spent 13 months in jail waiting for trial says, "You know what happens to an animal when you put it in a hole? The animal tries and tries and tries every way to get out but when it finds out it can't get out

it just settles down and accepts and adjusts.

"You can't live two places at the same time."

Prisoners on this tier have been accused of murder, rape, armed robbery.

All day is spent cleaning and cleaning and cleaning the tier, watching TV, playing cards, discussing each other's sad stories, life histories, raps, complaining, pacing up and down, listening to the radio, smoking cigarettes, staring at the walls, writing letters, counting the hours, waiting for the mail, waiting, waiting, waiting, worrying, worrying, worrying, wishing, wishing, wishing, complaining, dreaming of the streets, existing, reading, arguing, and for some of the prisoners climbing on top the top bunk of the jail cell to talk to the women prisoners three floors up through the air vent, carrying on a hot verbal romance.

The romances are very hot and the thrill of rapping to a woman's voice is exciting.

The day is organized around meals and each day is marked by a small schedule change that distinguishes it from another day. To constantly think of the outside and dream of hitting the bricks soon is to subject your soul to constant harassment and soul self-torture. Prisoners are treated like infants.

Everyone feels sorry for themselves till he hears the next guy's rap.

Young white youth stand on the dawn of history because he/she is without a culture and without a past.

Nothing in the past gives us anything to build on.

The history of the white man has been a history of plunder and theft and

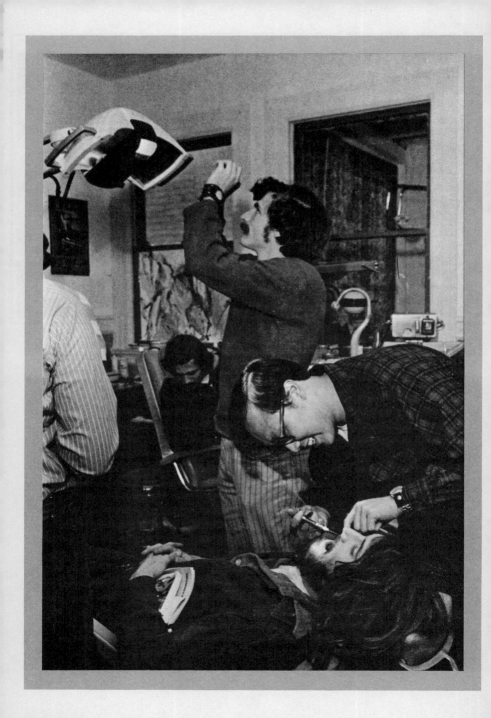

the construction of religions and value systems which justify this rape.

Finally the technological atomic age arrives and we are the first leisure babies. We are supposed to enjoy these comforts but we can only feel shame.

Our schools are shells to keep us busy.

We have nothing to do but colonize the natives (blacks, yellows) who may become crazy enough to demand back what was stolen from them!

The religions of the past, Catholic, Christian, Jewish, are hypocritical creeds used to justify white man's murder and to confuse the poor. We are all refugees from Catholicism, Protestantism, Judaism. We come to each other anew to create a new religion of the streets.

The culture of the urban middle class is mechanical plastic and without passion.

Black youth must redeem the culture stolen from them and relate to their history of suffering.

But they have something real.

We white youth—without a culture, a past, heroes to respect and model, or any traditions stand at freedom's door.

We refuse to be spare parts in the technological bureaucratic machine.

We refuse to be half-human. We know that our history begins with our birth.

We owe no obligation to the past or to our parents.

We must create our own morality and way of life. We are not interested in material security while three-quarters of the world is starving. We are secure enough to seek a life of insecurity.

We dig Thoreau's statement that the free woman and free man can leave the burning city naked.

Fuck material possessions!

We are erasing the absurd racial and religious differences which have divided the world.

We do not learn in school.

School turns us into intellectuals, driven by guilt. We do not experience life in school. We do not learn the skills necessary for survival. We learn more from a daily newspaper than we do from any school book. High school and college train us psychologically to be word machines, intellects without experience. School is a place where society brainwashes its children with the lies of the past.

We must teach ourselves.

We must learn from our sisters and brothers in life experience.

We learn by doing.


It was July 4th and the jail was letting us outside for a variety show. I sat down next to another longhair and we began rapping. He's in jail for sale of LSD. "The FBI just came to see me," he says, "about my brother who got killed at Kent State. I keep asking them which National Guardsman killed my brother but they keep asking me who burned down the ROTC building."

You never know who you'll meet out at the yard at Cook County Jail.

This is Ken, brother of Jeff Miller, one of the four beautiful young people murdered by the National Guard at Kent. Ken is bushy-haired and a veteran, unfortunately, of many prisons although only twenty-one years old.

When he was seventeen years old he was hitch-hiking from L.A. to Chicago. He got picked up by three guys.

In Albuquerque the cops stopped the car for speeding and found out it was a stolen car. They arrested all four kids in the car, including Ken.

"But I was only hitch-hiking," Ken said.

Nobody believed Ken was only hitch-hiking. Ken got sentenced to the Youth Act, six months to six years, an indeterminate sentence, depending on how long it takes them to break you, and he served two years.

He got out, saw his brother killed at Kent, was busted for possession of LSD, had his parole revoked and was sent back to the joint.

Above all Amerika fears the dope pusher.

The combination of dope and revolutionary politics is a killer, but dope usually comes first. In 1966 Tim Leary toured the country telling kids to turn on with dope, recreate their own environment, be born anew. He upset the politicos because he also said protesting was a game, politics a bad trip, and everything important happens in your head. In a way Leary was reflecting his own generational bias. Our theories can come only out of our experience, and Leary had never personally experienced the turn-on beauty and ecstasy of a campus demonstration or confrontation.

But Leary was the major recruiter for campus battles.

All campus struggles begin in the home in the revolt against parental monarchy.

Leary was a home wrecker.

Oming will never destroy the bars of any prison.

The revolution begins in your head but it takes reality in the streets. "Good vibes" can be just another form of Amerikan middle-class empty-headed cheerfulness. No sadder sight than to see a white middle-class person straight out of the plastic suburbs, never victim of pig brutality, saying blacks should be "nonviolent and peaceful" and change their own heads.

Some hippies feel superior to blacks because they think they're beyond the "subject-object violence game." You know, the garbage that says that there is no difference between Rap Brown and John Mitchell. They are all caught in a you-versus-me violence trip and should seek a higher unity in their own heads.

"You can be free if you want to be."

Such pacifism is ruling-class garbage.

For white middle-class hippies to say that is to express the same racism of a Southern white, only more subtle, less blatant, a "superiority" to black people and a refusal to see a difference between the oppress*or* and oppress*ed*.

I've met many hippies who consider themselves superior to black people because "We are living the future!"

Hippies who've "dropped out of politics" have dropped out of life, dropped out of their own ability to feel and experience the sufferings of others. Pill-dropping parents escape to the suburbs; pot-smoking hippies escape to the "country."

No freak will be free until Bobby Seale is free.

I don't mean all hippies who go to the country—some go to escape; others go to train militarily, spiritually, psychologically, politically for the coming civil war. Some want to be left alone; others are trying new models for human relations away from the pressures of urban life.

We are going to have to learn to create our utopias on the barricades.

**ALL HIPPIES MUST BECOME YIPPIES.**

A yippie is a hippie international revolutionary.

Some hippies are arrogant and put down Cuba for bad vibes; yippies respect the problems and struggles of other liberation struggles.

Our liberation struggle comes out of affluence and security—we must learn to relate to liberation struggles which come out of poverty and insecurity.

We should respect their militancy discipline and they should respect our dope. We'll give them dope and they'll teach us discipline.

The yippie liberation struggle is the women's liberation struggle is the Vietnamese liberation struggle is the black liberation struggle is the South African liberation struggle. No one can succeed without all of them succeeding.

Individually, Amerika might be able to militarily or economically destroy one struggle: together we got Amerika up against the wall!


## CONFIDENTIAL COMMUNICATION
## BETWEEN ME (J. RUBIN) AND MY
## LAWYER, RONALD J. CLARK


**Wednesday, July 15**


The revolution is nothing if it is not spiritual but the spiritual revolution by itself is nothing.

Ministers of the spirit are usually phonies: the spirit will sanction anything. Spiritual revolution and psychedelic capitalism go hand-in-hand.

God and money go hand-in-hand.

Any dope smoker is a hypocrite who gets high without fighting to free dope-political martyr John Sinclair. I hope next time they smoke they don't get high! Alcoholics are cynics and individuals; pot smokers are lovers and dreamers who create a new society. Tim Leary and John Sinclair are, like Bobby Seale, prisoners of war.

But it's odd. Sometimes it is more difficult to get people to fight for themselves than to fight for others.

This is self-hate in those dope-smoking hippies and lefties who demand that Bobby Seale be set free but who ignore Sinclair. We got to fight for Sinclair just like we fight for Bobby. We got to accept the fact that we are an oppressed minority too.

Dope is political because it is our sacrament.

Often it's easy to protest *someone else's oppression.* End the war! Free Bobby! It's harder, especially for white middle-class youth who feel guilt and shame over their skin, to protest our own oppression.

Whites are oppressed because they are crippled from birth by security and plastic environment money and overintellectualism and pride and they don't even know they are oppressed. The Viet Cong and Panthers are making themselves free by fighting but whites are overwhelmed by fear and lives without meaning. Young whites have got to free themselves.

Liberals help other people's struggles.

Revolutionaries fight for our own freedom.

We got to free the children of the suburbs. We got to free the prisoners in high schools and colleges of Amerika. We are an oppressed colony, a new

nation. We got to overcome our own guilt and self-hate which blinds us to our own oppression.

Amerika gasps—rightly so!—when Russia puts its dissidents into insane asylums. But what about all the kids who have been put into mental hospitals by their parents for "flipping out"?

Open the mental institutions!

Free the schools! Open the jails!

Housewives are political prisoners.

Children are political prisoners!

Secretaries are political prisoners.

Just because our parents physically reproduced us doesn't mean they "own" us like property or something. We belong to ourselves. We can choose our own destiny.

Self-determination for children!

Children of Catholic parents are rejecting Catholicism! Parents have no innate right to push their religion or prejudices or way of life upon children, babies. They have superior power and babies are helpless.

They have no moral right.

Parents try to relive their broken lives through their kids. But freaks with our magical lifestyles have through the power of the media reached into every home and romanticized and reached children and declared war on parents and given young kids a new alternative!

Child molesters!

Home wreckers!

Child liberators!

Dope and hair and Woodstock and demonstrations are part of the new life, and kids should run away from home at an early age and form communes and live in youth ghettos.

Parents get what they deserve. They are the victims of children's liberation. If they acted like kids too, we would turn them on—we are not vindictive—but most parents are dictators passing on dead lifeless traditions.

*To impose your way of life on your children is the worst ego trip of all.*

We, the first generation to revolt, will not have an antagonistic split with our kids. We reject the idea of the private home and nuclear family and we believe kids should be raised communally with other kids and with many different models, not just one "mother" or "father." We have no vested interests to defend against the next generation.

Generational revolt is not automatic. It broke out in the 1960's because the revolution began in the sixties. We are not going to impose on our kids what we rejected as kids. As "parents" we refuse to "grow up"—so we know what it's like to be kids. Our kids are our equals—we are taking acid, flipping out with our kids!

Freedom in America is "growing up" and becoming a "mother" or "father" and oppressing your kids.

Our kids raise and teach us!

Kids under eighteen are considered runaways and parents hire headhunters to raid our communities dragnetting for the "runaways." But we are all runaways! We must drive all the foreign elements out of our communities from undercover rats to FBI agents—never, never speak to an FBI agent—to heroin pushers to money-greed capitalists to ROTC death merchants.

The pigs on college campuses and off-campus communities are as illegitimate as the white pigs in the black ghettos and the Amerikan soldiers in Vietnam. They do not live in the communities they police, they do not speak the language; they do not respect or honor the local customs or traditions, they are representatives of an outside, immoral, illegal foreign power trying to impose its will on us, whether we are young whites, blacks or Vietnamese.

As well as juries of our peers we want "pigs-of-our-peers."

In one of the weirdest electoral campaigns in modern history A.C. (After Chicago), yippie Stew Albert ran for sheriff of Alameda County in the spring of 1970 under the campaign slogan: "Elect a Peoples' Pig!" Stew centered his campaign around conditions of Santa Rita; he rapped with visitors who came to visit prisoners every weekend.

Stew had just served three months inside and he was getting revenge for his sisters and brothers still locked up. He got 65,000 votes, 30 per cent—

*New York City*

# THIS IS IT

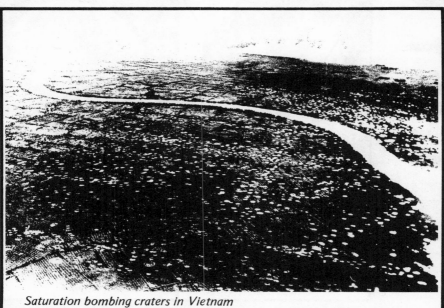

*Saturation bombing craters in Vietnam*

The Rockefeller boys

Charles Engelhard

Frederick Kappel

THEY OWN IT

(l. to r.): Hoover, Mitchell, Nixon, McClelland, Kleindeinst

The Joint Chiefs of Staff

THEY POLICE IT

shocking the pigs! We'll see how much respect they have for the "democratic process" when we start winning elections.

Full-scale military police Nazism will probably come to this country after real liberals and radicals win elections—and the business class and police take over power and off the election.

"Elections" are merely a game to keep the people distracted.

Real power in America is wielded by people you never elect and most of the time don't even see—powerful businessmen and the police. The "vote" is meaningless when up against the secret police, the FBI, "Red Squads" of all police professional military departments—not to mention the CIA.

The "politician" serves the businessman and the police. That's why it is naïve to believe that we can change Amerika through elections.

Politics in Amerika is just an extension of Hollywood—the world of distraction.

A "political" strategy for taking over without a military strategy is a program for fascism.

"Liberals" who believe the CIA killed Kennedy have not learned the lesson of his blood. We gotta build an army.

### Thursday, July 16

The more successful the liberals are, the greater the danger of fascism—unless revolutionaries are preparing by creating armed, liberated communities, revolutionary political consciousness and an international strategy.

The election of a "peace president" will invite a right-wing coup—the dawn of firing squads, concentration camps and a military-police-business takeover unless we are prepared to prevent it.

Business and police are not going to give up their power nonviolently—they can always scare up a "national security crisis" to cancel elections, suspend civil liberties, take over the media and put us away.

Our protection lies in our ability to hurt them more than they can hurt us. Our protection lies in the extent to which we are armed—militarily, economically, spiritually.

Hippie pacifism will be the ideology of the victims of Nazism.

Our protection may lie in the speed with which China develops the H-bomb and gives us a nuclear umbrella.

Our survival is at stake.

Our strength lies in our unity, our sisterhood and brotherhood, our ability not to be divided. If they take one, they must try and take all. If they can take us one by one, group by group, they'll have us all pretty easily.

Those people who are not in the camps will be out because of their tacit acceptance of the jailing of others.

The price of freedom will be turning one's head.

The price of freedom will be saying, "I'm different."

We got a frightening glimpse of this when Leary and Sinclair were jailed. Leary's jailing without appeal bond was practically a secret. The media blacked it out. College students ignored it because "It's not my issue."

Friends close to Tim took an attitude psychologically necessary for their own stability but politically disastrous: Don't worry; Tim will be out very soon, the higher courts will give him bond, we got the law on our side.

So the crisis was off.

Adrenalin stopped flowing. People relaxed: trust the "higher" courts.

We began hearing from Tim's stoned acid friends that it was a good thing for Tim that he was in jail! "If he's there, that's where he should be." The universal Karma. Tim's ex-partner, ex-dope peddler Richard Alpert, who saved his skin by becoming a medicine man in India, actually told a couple of hundred hippie mystics at a media conference in Vermont: "Tim is in jail because that's his Karma. Trust and obey your Karma, grow with it."

No anger, just peace.

Tim's hippie following had repudiated organization. So there were no offices, demonstrations, rallies for Tim.

The powerful figures in the dope-rock world showed themselves to be phonies in the midst of the crisis. Crisis tests men's and women's souls and reveals truth. John Lennon could have organized massive international rallies and rock festivals for Tim yet he didn't even send a penny.

A lot of acid heads suddenly became closet acid heads.

I took a mescaline trip one day and freaked out.

I felt all around me desperation, hate, fear, repression, death. It was getting so that for a political revolutionary *how you die* was becoming more important than *how you live.* Reading the underground press at that time was hard because it seemed to spread the idea of preparing ourselves to die: Break up monogamy. Love is dead. Romance is over. Criticize yourself incessantly. Individuality is bourgeois. All nonviolence is bullshit. Bombs, guns, bombs.

The definition of revolutionary was becoming: bomber. And an escalating pattern appeared: Bomb, go underground. No other activity—from rock concerts to guerrilla theater to a peaceful march—seemed revolutionary.

We were all criticizing and attacking one another so much that in my mescaline-heightened sensitivity I saw all of us on one big death trip. The revolution was being defined as physical and nothing more. Che became the symbol—and why? Because he died in battle.

*Only the dead can be heroes.*

In the middle of the mescaline trip the phone rang. I picked it up and it was Abbie. "Tim Leary just escaped from prison! He climbed over the wall!" Abbie said. I must have jumped 100 feet in the air with joy. Jail escape! Tim Leary! He wasn't going to rot away in jail. How did he do it? I kept wondering.

We went over to the offices of the *East Village Other* where they debated what kind of a picture of Leary to put on the cover: a serious picture or a smiling laughing one? Some of the staff wanted the serious picture. I argued for the laughing one.

While Leary was telling all of us he liked jail, he was planning his escape. What a joke he played on the world!

But how?

I went to sleep wondering how the fuck he did it.

The next day Leary announced that the Weather Underground had planned and executed his escape from prison. He added: "I am armed and should be considered dangerous." My mind literally exploded. I could not hold back tears of happiness. The union of Weatherman and LSD, the internal and external revolution.

What a great action—freeing Tim Leary! While no one else cared—while liberals, college students, professors and the nonviolent hippie establishment accepted the fact of Leary in jail—the Weatherpeople acted.

Leary decided the first second he entered jail that he was going to escape. He said to the press, "You can't jail love," and he meant it literally, not symbolically.

He spent three hours a day doing sit-ups and push-ups, lifting weights, doing isometric exercises with the magic bullworker and playing handball to get his wrists and arms in shape to scale over the wall.

He decided to con the authorities to get moved out of isolation.

He wrote letters to Ronald Reagan, senators, congressmen and newspapers saying he didn't mind jail but could he please get into minimum security to read and write?

He spent hours surveying the wall at San Luis Obispo and checking the exact hours that guards went on and off work. To avoid the danger of snitches among the prisoners, he smiled all the time, telling everyone he'd be getting out on bail any day now—thereby avoiding suspicion as he measured the jail walls.

He never complained—he was always smiling and happy.

It took Leary eight months, but he was ready. Leary knew he faced certain death. California prison guards have an automatic "shoot-to-kill" order if they see prisoners trying to escape. Leary decided to gamble all.

He was going to try and go over the front wall in sight of guard towers and gun trucks and onto the main highway.

It had never been done before, and it was so obvious and dangerous no one would expect it.

Leary thought it was better to die trying to live rather than to live like a slave. A free animal cannot be free in jail, he said; your mind is not free if your body is not free.

*Leary decided to risk death—to live.*

For six months the Weatherpeople planned Leary's escape.

They moved into the small town of San. Luis Obispo. Their mission: Get

Leary out of that small town of 5,000 people and to a safe place and into a new identity without leaving any clues. FBI men would be swarming into town the next day looking for traces of Weatherman or Leary.

They had one understanding—no guns could be used, so there would be no deaths. They did not want to go into the prison guns ablazing to free Leary. They analyzed the prison, studied detailed escape routes for days and days— all the time while stoned. One mistake would mean death.

Leary took LSD and found a secret though dangerous way to climb over the 12-foot slanted barbed wire fence without being seen by the floodlights.

The Weatherpeople took LSD and picked him up on the highway in a car. Tim Leary, Rosemary Leary, Bernardine Dohrn and Jeff Jones went to see the far-out movie *Woodstock* stoned out of their minds.

John Sinclair was jailed because he is a powerful influence on young kids in Michigan using dope, music, art. Then in 1967 Sinclair's collective got turned on by the Black Panthers and the soul of their politics. For Sinclair, white rock-'n'-roll came through black blues and jazz. Blacks taught whites music.

So with politics.

Blacks suffered more so they are closer to truth and reality. Revolutionary whites relate to black soul politics the way white musicians relate to black soul musicians.

Politics and music are the same: expressions of human energy.

Here were leather-jacketed young whites reading and distributing the Black Panther Party paper, reading Mao's Red Book, smoking dope, learning to use guns, digging Eldridge and Huey and Bobby, living communally, and dancing and making rock-'n'-roll at the same time! Rap Brown is Jimi Hendrix is Billie Holiday is Fred Hampton.

What music those Panthers make!

Whites, without a culture of their own, took the soul and guts of black feeling and adapted it to their own reality.

The White Panthers was born and their origins were jazz and rhythm and blues and rock and the Black Panthers. They did not ask the Black Panthers for permission. They just did it.

*It is one of the beautiful, soulful ironies of history that the children of the oppressor achieve their freedom through learning from the oppressed.*

And so these freaks became White Panthers the way Janis Joplin became a blues singer.

The energy of the house was electronic, the driving beat of a rock band, the Mc5. It was a rare experience, this union of rock band, collective living and political center. The music gave the Panthers a way to reach thousands of teen-agers; the politics gave the band a myth and energy. Runaways off the street were embraced at the White Panther communal house. At the same

time certain symbolic centers of Pig Amerika in the nearby vicinity were blown up.

The White Panthers were madness with vision, a glimpse of the revolutionary future, flower children at day, urban guerrillas at night. They lived, ate, slept together, exploring new ways of living together.

But the pigs were laying a deep trap for these psychedelic revolutionaries. A long-haired pig set up a head shop and allegedly bummed a roach from John Sinclair. Those were the naïve unparanoid beautiful free moments of hippie history.

The barbaric laws of Michigan make possession a crime demanding 10 years of one's life. John Sinclair was found guilty.

In one of the piggiest moments of USA injustice the judge denied Sinclair appeal bond and jailed him.

The Mc5, seeing that things were going bad, deserted the White Panthers and went their commercial way. The soul went out of their music and was replaced with money.

Higher courts turned down Sinclair's appeal on the grounds that he was a menace to society. So John Sinclair languishes in jail. All that energy bottled up in one tiny spot.

John Sinclair is not in jail for pot. John Sinclair is in jail for child molesting. His electronic power of reaching young kids had to be cut.

John Sinclair is in jail because he is too powerful to be free.

Meanwhile the pigs were leveling in on Pun Plamondon, the Minister of Defense of the White Panthers. Pun faced 20 years on a Traverse City, Michigan, dope beef. One day he turned on the radio to hear that he had just been indicted by the federal government for blowing up a CIA building. He rushed to a friend's house to hide.

Within a few hours he was in a car leaving Ann Arbor and Michigan, never again to visit his commune, lovers, friends, home.

He was underground.

Five months later J. Edgar Hoover paid Pun the greatest compliment the USA government can pay one of its citizens: Pun was moved to the Top 10 of the FBI's Most Wanted List.

Although the White Panthers are in Ann Arbor, they hardly organized at the University of Michigan campus; therefore there was nary a peep when John was taken away and Pun driven underground and accidentally later captured.

The campuses are our base and where we can have some leverage over the powerful in Amerika.

When John and Pun were jammed, the University of Michigan should have burned and fallen—setting off a chain reaction of fallen dominoes across the country. The isolation of nonstudent freakout centers from large campus bases is very dangerous; it is like separating the fish from the sea.

In our communities the state will wither away and the repressive arm of authority will be replaced by self-governing individuals and communes.

Sharing will be the means of exchange.

Amerika operates under the sick idea that if each individual seeks her or his own self-interest, the result will be collective good. Jive!

Professional police therefore are needed to protect the property and privilege of the haves from the have-nots, and jails are needed to isolate and punish the have-nots.

In a yippie society everyone will seek both their own self-interest and the good of the community because the rat race will be *over*.

Money will become useless pieces of toilet paper as the necessities of life are free and shared.

Work will be done as artistic expression and for human solidarity.

Decisions will be made by people in action.

The parasites of the community, landlords, owners, businessmen, will be made to *work* for a living!

The "police" will be replaced by the militia of all the people.

We are the children of technology and we know that if you can blow up the world and go to the moon you can do anything.

So help me, if I have to sprout wings I'm going to the moon and rip that fuckin' Amerikan flag off there!

No country has the right to put its flag on the moon! We're going into space for military reasons to spy on China. We should redirect all that energy and bread that we're using on missiles, Vietnam, war, moon, and use it to guarantee every human being on this planet a human life.

The technology is oppressing us. Technology is just a lot of toys anyway.

Take those toys away from the kill-greed creeps.

The battle of the revolution in Amerika is a fight for control and use of the toys. In 1970 anything is possible. Our technology is today being used for nonhuman purposes. Our technology violates our human nature.

We want *everything* for *everybody*.


Pretty soon I begin to realize that when I meet someone there are usually three people there: me, the other person and the person's image of me.

In jail I experienced it the most weirdly.

The guard on the outside ballfield said he'd try to bring me outside every day. The deputy warden said no—I was too "famous." The guard wanted to bring me out special 'cause I was Jerry Rubin and was prohibited especially from bringing me out 'cause I'm Jerry Rubin!

The screw giving me a hard time, putting me through finger-printing and picture-taking—making me feel miserable—pauses to ask me for my autograph.

One of the leaders of the Black P. Stone Nation was on the same tier I was on. Suddenly after two weeks the deputy warden arrived and ordered him to pack up. Why? "We can't have you and Jerry Rubin on the same tier," he said. The Stone was moved up to the hole and put on double lock. "It was just an excuse—they wantd to get him," the other Stones said.

Everybody sees me as JERRY RUBIN but I know I'm just Jerry Rubin. I have trouble dealing with people's expectations of me. Jerry Rubin will probably be assassinated someday, and I'll bleed bad.


It's weird getting recognized by strangers on the street. I dig it.

Being a celebrity is a powerful weapon—people listen to you and tell other people stories about you.

You are myth.

You are media.

Usually by the time the story moves it has little if anything to do with you as a person, but deals with other people's fears, prejudices and fantasies.

Friends don't do it maliciously but when they are with you they don't see *you.* I don't mean close friends, I mean acquaintances. I try to break that down because I am really a shy, quiet, gentle, soft person. But it doesn't work, because that's against my myth.

"Hey, you're supposed to be Jerry Rubin! Speak up! Do something!" people say to me.

When I meet people I like to listen, not talk. It's tough—I can't participate in any demonstration or riot unless completely disguised. Pigs head straight to nab me—and young kids hang around me seeking me to lead them in rock-throwing and barricade-building.

I've discovered that my presence either starts or stalls a riot: I can't be just

*part* of a crowd. If I do nothing people will stand around watching me and waiting—if I move people join. "What should *we* do?" I'm asked over and over—a question that is too much for one individual.

I hear Spiro Agnew, Herbert Klein, Ronnie Reagan, S. I. Hayakawa mention "Jerry Rubin" and I wonder: Who the hell are they talking about? What fierce image comes to their mind? They're not talking about *me*—they're relating to *the image* in their heads.

To keep my sanity I must remember the difference between myself and my image. Image is a powerful political weapon. Images battle—not real people.

"Jerry Rubin" now frightens liberals, parents, professors—and inspires young kids, so it is a positive image. The task is to use the celebrity status for the revolution.

If ever it becomes a non- or counterrevolutionary image, I'll change my name. My image is somewhat out of my hands now, out of control.

I've become a symbol. My goal is to accept my responsibility as a leader—'cause leaders are necessary, and *everyone* should become a leader—and to grow with it.

The gap between the real person and the image can't get too far.

I can't do anything noncontroversial any more.

Danger comes when people are unaware of difference between image and person, but movement celebrities like me, Abbie, etc., are forever torn apart, asked embarrassing questions, put on the spot, laughed at, loved, hated, knocked down. Believe me, there are many times when we want to drop out.

173

We are considered public property.

If we're with friends in a restaurant, other people feel they have every right to come up and bring up any subject any time, no matter how personal. I get annoyed but I also love it. People have every right: *I am public.*

Which reminds me of a quote, in an interview with Janis Joplin, that I copied out of a newspaper some months ago:

> People expect Janis Joplin to be a tough bitch, and say I start talking to them like a lonely little girl—that's not in their image of me—they don't see it. Say you meet somebody you've heard about, you don't ever see them, you don't see who they are and who they need to be recognized as, you see who you need them to be. . . .
> Being famous makes it a lot harder. People don't talk to you like people any more, they just want to know if you know Mick Jagger or something.

The contrast in New Haven is incredible: on one side street absolute barbarism, a legal lynching, the planned execution of eight black men and women through the most sophisticated legal means, but in essence no more complicated than a group of whites with ropes around their arms rushing out to hang some niggers up on a tree.

Across the street stands Yale, the peak of intellectualism, where intellectuals do their work without seeing the lynching and violence down the street.

If you bury your head in your books, you won't hear the screams of the niggers down the street.

So intellectuals concentrate on their tiny problems and never see the daily crimes of murder committed by police and businessmen against black people.

The "ivory tower" and the jails can even be across the street from each other!

On the highest levels the same people who control Yale also control those courtrooms!

Western culture and barbarism mix. The universities are other forms of jails with the prisoners—professors and students—there on the promise they won't attack the rich and powerful who control everything.

Blacks should invade college campuses, waking up intellectuals and students to the reality and bitterness of daily life in Amerika. Poor black people should teach intellectuals and M.A.'s and Ph.D.'s what's going down in this country.

There is more wisdom on *any* jail tier in any county jail or penitentiary in Amerika than in any lecture hall in any university.

The schools are islands of white culture where intellectuals talk to intellectuals—blind leading the blind—while in another part of the campus real people plan germ warfare, containment of revolution, atomic research and more sophisticated means to control black, brown, red and yellow people.

The intellectuals aren't supposed to be too nosey about what's going on outside the library.

Mind your own intellectual business! And so the universities ostensibly are places where civilized white society passes on its intellectual tradition to others, while keeping out the savages and the poor—the feared "outside agitators."

But it is the suffering "savages" who must liberate our universities to the truth of Amerika.

Everything is upside down.

The "savages" are civilized—the civilized run a savage society in suits and ties and "rational" discussions of "legal" means.

It took the civil rights movement to wake up the sleeping campuses.

It took the Viet Cong to breathe life and spirit and action into the campuses.

It takes oppressed blacks and poor and criminals to liberate white and "Negro" college youth from their blind fearful castrated intellectual professors.

And that's why the Black Panthers and The Conspiracy came to Yale for the Free Bobby May Day rally.

Truth comes from one's life experiences—not through ideas or books. The savages must civilize us. The uneducated must teach us truth. The young must show us right and wrong.

Masses of ghetto youth and prisoners should march on campuses to tell inmates there what is happening.

Just the rumor of the Panthers coming had a profound effect. Impending winds of revolution storming from all over to "take over" Yale forced the students to look in a mirror. A month before May Day the Law School and other departments went on strike.

One of the purposes had been achieved without our even going there—the fear was enough.

Yale president Kingman Brewster saw his campus in flames on May 1. He realized that if Yale opposed the May Day rally, Yale might become the object of the fury of the revolutionaries. If Yale opened its doors to the rally, cancelled classes for a while, then there would be no reason for the radicals to attack Yale and the rally might come and go—an exercise in American civil liberties.

It was brilliant ruling-class thinking.

Yale would even provide room and board for its guests! Yale students would work as monitors to guard against violence. The pigs would help Brewster by mobilizing the National Guard and paratroopers and napalm so that the guests would feel so overwhelmed by this display of state power that they would be happy to get out of town alive.

Containment.

Brewster reasoned that the event would have less impact if it passed peacefully than if there was an incident.

Brewster did this because *we* frightened him more than the right-wing pigs frightened him—his capitulation was a sign of our power.

This strategy was not disastrous for us in its end result because the political goal of the Panthers at that time was to dramatize the trial and make it national, throw a spotlight on New Haven, make Bobby Seale a household word again and begin a series of actions.

Teach-ins precede riots.

The Black Panthers are very political and careful in their decisionmaking. However, the weekend was a huge down because of the way it happened, revealing a split in the white-black movements that theory cannot breach, and that must be resolved by mutual respect and separate actions.

For whites, street actions are a way of toughening ourselves up.

Riots are an appropriate response to the level of repression now existing on campuses and in white communities; riots are an appropriate physical response to psychological oppression and in rioting young people form gangs and collectives, learn trust and comradeship, practice street-fighting skills, expose state violence and begin to define a community turf.

Blacks already have defined their community and turf.

Through riots whites begin to arm themselves.

Blacks are already armed.

Whereas riots *may* be suicidal in the black community because the pigs feel they have the moral authority and support automatically to open fire on a black mob, whites are still somewhat protected by their white skins and have a lot more rioting to do before the pigs automatically open fire.

Besides, riots are great theater.

Riots have replaced baseball as the national pastime.


So thousands of tough young whites arrived in New Haven with clubs, pipes, and helmets, matches and fantasies of listening to speeches by day and rioting at night.

It's interesting—each area has its own style of street fighting. In Santa Barbara all is peaceful during the day. Guerrillas look like ordinary students or freaks. Then night falls and the peasants become Viet Cong. The town burns.

In Berkeley the riots take place in broad daylight and continue into the night.


To the Panthers this seemed fucked up—young white kids without guns, marching against *armed* police.

As night fell I was giving a workshop to about 1,500 people on campus. The bullhorn wasn't working and I was exhausted and beat and didn't feel

like rapping and a black guy asked to speak, said he was a Panther (he wasn't) and that people had been arrested on the green and what were we going to do about it?

I was torn, because I dig riots but I thought the Panthers had the right to decide what went down this weekend because it was their trial and they called the demonstration.

"Oh shit," I thought, "I'll get blamed for this!" as I saw 1,000 warriors racing to the green and into battle. I took the bullhorn to say I was opposed to the action but it was gone.

For the next five hours on the green the most amazing sight struck our eyes—Black Panthers and conservative-liberal Yale students with bullhorns together ordering wide-eyed radicals off the streets, out of battle and back into "your houses."

The Panthers called the white rioters "agents provocateurs" and said rioting was a fool's game.

"Don't go up against the Man with bricks and bottles! He's got guns! Go home and get yourself a gun! Defend yourself! A revolutionary has a gun! Don't go up against the Man unless you have a gun too!"

After verbal battles between young whites and Panthers, the streets were cleared although the campus choked of tear gas.

That was some achievement.

*No demonstration is complete without some tear gas.*

But the feeling in the pit of one's stomach was worse than the burning gas in our eyes. The Panthers were right to police their demonstration if they wanted to, but the Panthers cannot be the leaders of the whole movement. No automatic applications can be made from black to white communities.

For blacks—I am not about to give black people advice how to fight their struggle—defending yourself in your home with a gun may be the revolutionary lifestyle. But young whites cannot wait for the pigs to come to our homes because they will never come.

We must go on the offensive, liberating territory and taking over universities.

If the goal is a black and white revolutionary army with guns, how will that be achieved? Not by telling whites to get guns. Whites will get guns when they have to, when there is no other choice, when they're up against the wall.

To tell whites to go home and get guns is to tell whites to do nothing.

It's another example where an extreme left-wing strategy leads to conservation and inaction.

A gun does not make someone a revolutionary.

Rioting is a necessary step to the day when whites are armed with guns.

*A match, a rock, a brick, a Molotov cocktail, dynamite, dope, a printing press, a picket sign and a pair of feet are also revolutionary props today.*

The Panthers put down the wild chaos and anarchy of the street fighting, calling for us to build a disciplined, organized party.

For blacks, organizing is essential because black communities are anarchic and dominated by organized white people.

Blacks must create and build an organization of their own. But young whites have escaped from the overorganized society and for us anarchy is freedom. We got a lot of shit to stir, and anarchy produces chaos and stirs up the shit.

Within the "do it!" anarchy, survival forces us to form collectives and

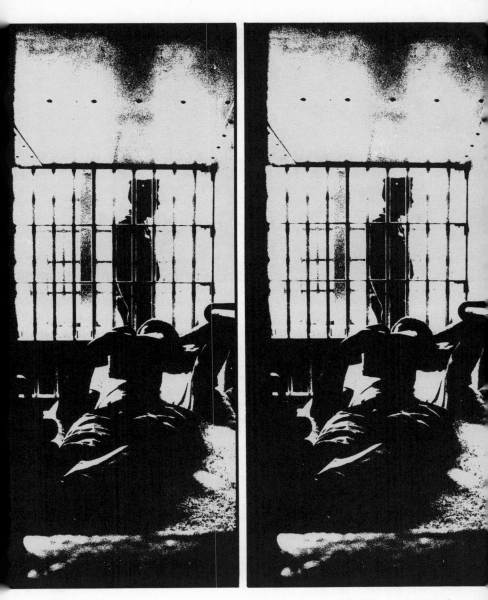

communes—our basic form of organization. Repression will push us to higher forms of organization—but the organizing without the need for it could hold back the free energy of youth.

The Panthers have problems with action freaks—we have problems with nonviolence and abstract intellectuals and liberals. Therefore different styles and organizations are needed—at this stage of the revolution.

Anarchy, as Eldridge said, is a tactic.

And when action—any action—is needed, anarchy is the best tactic.

The next day another huge rally was scheduled and I was to speak. The Panthers asked me to "cool it." I am psychologically incapable of giving a "cool it" speech. I was torn and I wanted to get out of speaking, but that was a cop-out. So I asked to speak first so later speakers could calm the crowd if I accidently excited it. My main anger was with Kingman Brewster 'cause he had become the hero of the day.

It's important for these colleges to close and be taken over by us—not for college presidents to become heroes.

Brewster coopted the day. I began to lead the 50,000 people in a "FUCK YOU KINGMAN BREWSTER" chant—but I couldn't remember his name. Kingman BREWER, I thought it was. Previous FUCK YOU chants worked great with George Wallace at the Tennessee State House steps and Sam Yorty at Los Angeles City Hall. But here after a minute the crowd rejected the chant and turned it into FREE BOBBY SEALE!

That was outasight too.

I disappeared off the podium stage and into the crowd and me, Abbie, Anita and Nancy hitch-hiked back to New York.

A very weird weekend was over.

Richard Nixon's public relations aides studied the Yale demonstration. They took notes and learned. The following weekend the unwashed were planning to descend on the White House 100,000 strong to protest the USA invasion of Cambodia and the murder of four sisters and brothers at Kent State.

*Washington has always seemed so vulnerable.*

It's in the middle of the country and within hours thousands of people can pour in from many Eastern and Middle West cities and campuses. The ghetto is right there, ready to burn.

The White House sits in the middle of the city inviting a guerrilla attack.

The campuses had suddenly fallen like dominoes one after another and millions of straight college students had moved into the streets. Amerika was a mass uproar unlike anything yet experienced here and people were sniffing a Paris 1968. Revolutionaries were shocked by it all.

In *Do It!* I wrote, "If 100 campuses closed on the same day, we'd force the President of the United States to the conference table."

Well, it happened! Everyone was moving! Energy was focusing on Washington. The VC were soon to open up an offensive at 16th and Pennsylvania.

If Washington goes, Amerika itself looks like a sinking ship.

The international student revolution and general strike is under way.

Nixon called in his best counterinsurgency experts. All-out war in the Capital would be too much while the USA was off escapading in Cambodia, and he couldn't take another Kent State. Nixon needed time.

*The Manhattan House of Detention for Men*

He had to create the image of being a reasonable man.

The government had to appear firm but willing to listen to dissent. It would *kill* Asian revolutionaries but it would *listen* to Amerikan dissenters. So Nixon decided not to oppose the demonstration, but to take it over, to make it his demonstration. If handled well, the demonstration could make Nixon look good, the government appear open, and take the steam and energy out of the student strike.

He had to create *an image* of protest, peaceful petition. A government which listens, dialogue; not open confrontation and war between government and Amerikan citizens.

If successful, the demonstration would be a safety valve for demonstrators and strengthen the national image of the Nixon government.

Most important, to influence the majority of demonstrators would be to create the *image* of peace and negotiations and cooperation and legal protest *before* the demonstration took place.

Most demonstrations have leaders and leaders feel responsible and leaders can therefore be bought off.

The "leaders" then would be held responsible for the actions of the people and would move to control the demonstration.

*(The Tombs)*

Nixon would not have to police OR control the demonstration.

He would have the leaders of the demonstration police/control their own demonstration.

That would be much more effective. To gain this cooperation the government would have to let the dissenters have an area close to the White House—and then draw the line.

It would be easy.

The leaders of the Mobilization were all white middle-class secure rational men and women—much like Nixon. He was for the war and they were against it, but outside of that, they had a lot in common.

They didn't want chaos. He didn't. They had trouble with their kids. He did, too.

Together they had a common interest in keeping the demonstration cool, organized and disciplined, and in isolating the militants.

For the demonstration leaders, it was a numbers game. Bodies counted. The more thousands that came, the more impact the demonstration.

They want to believe in a democratic society where numbers influence policy because they have as much to fear and lose from a revolution as does Nixon. Besides, if the leaders were recalcitrant, and violence followed, the government would indict them.

So Nixon held a dove in one hand, and nightstick and gun in the other, as he went off to negotiate.

If only the Viet Cong would be so easy!

Nixon gave the demonstration leaders a little sandbox to play in right across from the White House.

The night before the demonstration he held a televised press conference, dominated by double-talk. Then at 5:30 A.M. he pulled the coolest move ever, a PR genius move.

He visited the demonstration area and chatted with demonstrators and moved freely among the young dissidents.

So the morning of the demonstration the headlines blared: NIXON VISITS DEMONSTRATORS. They talked about peace and he rapped about sports and surfing. Why didn't they scream at him? Get angry with him? Isn't a burned Vietnamese baby worth at least that?

Instead they helped him create his image of dialogue and reasonableness. Were they so taken in by meeting the President, a celebrity?

Such a meeting was a historic, symbolic encounter and the young people who met Nixon were representing all young people.

*By not spitting in his face, they let down our generation.*

That headline crushed the morale of the demonstrators.

The government put passenger buses around the White House as a polite barricade. Not tanks, no! Who can get angry at a bus? A ring of buses around the White House suggested a football game crowd.

The buses were the only inanimate object between the 100,000 people and Dick Nixon. In front of the buses stood lines of smiling Washington pigs. They didn't have to do much because in front of them stood "peace marshals," the new pacifist anti-war pigs who protected the White House from the rest of the demonstrators. Their armbands gave them power to tell other demonstrators what to do.

They told you to keep cool and be nonviolent and if you gave them backtalk they were ready to smack you in the jaw.

They were the sociologist's latest discovery: if you want to control a crowd, make some of the people pigs, give them authority symbols and a little power.

I thought our sisters and brothers were beyond that.

What's happened to our movement when we are divided against each other and some people can tell others what to do? Wherever you went there was a peace marshal telling you don't do that, you can't go there.

There must have been 5,000 of them.

They were flashing the V-sign and saying, "Give peace a chance," as they pushed you away from the direction of the White House and into the massive crowd under what felt like a 100-degree sun.

Pretty soon the police, temporarily unemployed, started giving V-signs too.

*They caught on quick.*

The whole day was marked by battles between marshals and demonstrators, and speeches. One boring speech after another. Every two-bit left organization and figure was getting their two-cent pay-off. Sometimes I think Nixon will surrender to halt the boredom. "I'll end the war if you just stop the speeches."

Only excitement of the day was when a right-winger nut grabbed the mike. We yippies rooted for him.

Bourgeois politicians and left bureaucrats and organizational mucky-mucks and other egos danced around on the stage. Mercifully the rally finally ended and the peace ("Give peace a chance") marshals directed the masses home.

As night fell the pigs got their kicks attacking the hairy people left and an incredible amount of trashing was done, unreported in the media, which had joined Nixon in this conspiracy to downplay violence and emphasize reason and national dialogue. The demonstration ended.

Nixon sighed, looked in the mirror and said: "What a bright fellow I am!"

*"I am the President!"*

Across the country peaceniks comforted themselves with the illusion that maybe their government favored peaceful dissent and listened to them. Meanwhile American soldiers moved into Cambodia in search of Asian revolutionaries to kill.

The heart went out of the student strike.

The crisis was over.

It was as if Nixon organized his own demonstration for his own image. Brilliant leaders try to create their own opposition.

The only exciting moment took place on Friday night at a predemonstration rally. For half an hour 10,000 freaks at the Washington Monument sat together and watched Maximum Leader doing his press conference on color TV, shouting obscenities at him, blowing grass, laughing, giving him *the finger* booing, laughing. Watching TV became a mass political act and the TV cameras filmed us watching Nixon on TV. The ultimate yippie act. What a trip!

When it was over, a gang of yippie guerrillas armed with clubs beat the TV into unconsciousness.

Our defense was a ball. Our goal was to have a good time in court and see our friends on the witness stand. The flow of witnesses reflected the differences among the defendants—we had no overall plan, but took turns bringing in our witnesses—yippie singing freaks with wild costumes followed Catholic priests who followed college professors, students, Justice Department officials, celebrities, housewives, then more crazy singers. Suspense dominated the room.

Lee Weiner buried himself in paperback books as if he was in the Northwestern University Library. The trial was just a distraction to his reading.

He read a book a day, only looked up when his name was occasionally mentioned and then to correct the pronunciation. When courtroom activities got a little too raucous, he buried himself deeper into the book.

It was his way of telling the courtroom that he was framed.

It got everybody uptight and became one of the most intriguing sights of the courtroom.

Lee was reading Zen and the trial flowed by.

Abbie was going to testify. His·wit is like a machine gun—just when you think you got him, he floors you with a one-liner.

Abbie has the best sense of absurdity I've ever seen and he can reduce the entire courtroom to absurdity. His mere Dennis the menace-bad little boy presence brings out the absurdity in everything. And we all know that revolutionaries are serious, revolutionaries don't laugh. Humor is a weapon—and Abbie's wild grin can even get the FBI laughing.

Abbie is superconscious of image and he knows it's hard for the government to jail someone who people think is *cute*.

He'll laugh their case to death.

Abbie had a lot of courage in courtroom because he was pure impulse, the politics of id and adolescence. To tame Abbie is a task for only the most masochistic repressor.

Yippies used pranks and humor and dope and long hair and all our other props as tactics to achieve our one true objective—the destruction of Imperialism.

## Saturday, July 18

Just as Abbie took the stand he felt down and not ready. So he discovered an illness—exaggerating a cough into some disease ending with "itis"—and fooled doctors, hospital officials, press, government doctors, judges, Julie, his own lawyers and even himself, stopping the trial for five days while he smoked dope and rested in his hospital bed watching color TV and dreaming up gimmicks for the stand, while banner front-page headlines day by day kept the people of Chicago in suspense over whether or not Abbie would survive his "yippie-pneumonia."

When he felt better, his disease was over and he came back to the witness stand and the trial resumed with jurors and press saying, "Hope you feel better, Mr. Hoffman."

He fooled the whole city and stopped the trial.

He returned to the stand from a wheelchair to a courtroom and city full of sympathy. He even got the Chicago *Sun-Times* to print a page-one picture of him with a tube over his face and his eyes closed. "Will Abbie pull through?"

After the photographer left, Abbie took the tube out of his mouth, took a puff of a joint and broke out in a belly laugh.

*That Abbie, he kills me.*

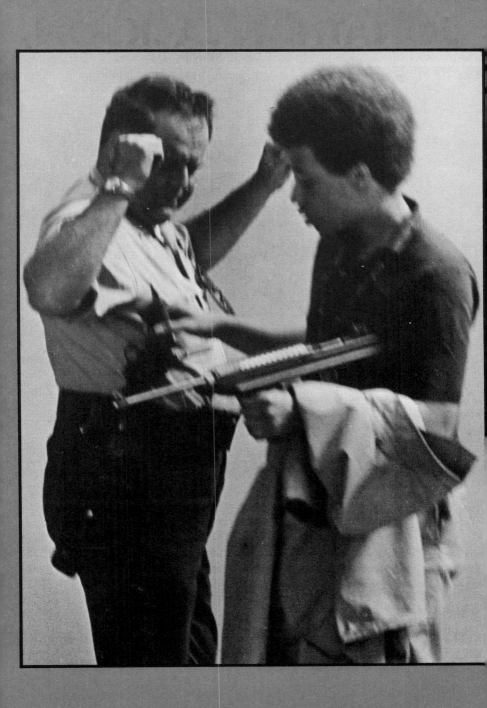

# JONATHAN JACKSON,

*August 8, 1970: Jonathan Jackson, William Christmas, John McClain, and Ruchell McGee took Marin County Judge Haley captive in an attempt to free*

# 1953-1970

*the Soledad Brothers from San Quentin prison. Jackson, Christmas, McClain and Haley were killed by the police.*

Music expresses the soul of our revolution.

The idea of going to Chicago and the Democratic convention in the first place was to bring our rock bands there—because with the rock bands come the people.

We wanted the jury to feel our music to understand us. Could we get the courtroom singing and dancing to the beat? We reach people not through rational political argument—but through the raw animal emotion of music.

Our culture was on trial because our culture attacked the convention in Chicago and our only hope was to turn the jury on to our music.

When you look at those sexless, emotionless creatures on the jury, you'd lose hope, but at least we'd go down singing. *Within every human adult there is a yippie sleeping.*

Could we grab the imagination of the jury?

Could we emotionally shock it into change?

Could we have in the courtroom the Festival of Life we were denied in Lincoln Park?

We were accused by the government of making nonnegotiable demands on the city—dope-smoking and public nudity and fucking and sleeping in Lincoln Park at night—to provoke the police to tear gas and club us, and then leading crowds in resisting the police as they tried to clear the park.

We argued, in defense, that we really wanted a festival in the park, we seriously sought permits and we did not advocate or lead crowds in violent defense of the park when attacked.

To dramatize our defense we brought to the stand the saints and minstrels of our culture.

We played back the eight months from December to August when we were organizing yippie and the festival, retelling the meetings, the pot parties, the dreams we had.

Our defense was far out!

We called to the stand as character witnesses Allen Ginsberg and Timothy Leary.

Ginsberg looks like Middle Amerika's nightmare of what awful things might happen to their kids—but on the stand Allen spoke directly to the jury in a calm, rational, considerate, explanatory, fatherly way—designed not to scare or frighten them but to put their minds at ease.

He tried to induce the jurors to grow as human beings, not to fear their bodies, to welcome and love their darkest and most repressed impulses, to accept the fact that whatever is human is divine and to realize that it is our technologically mad government that is inhuman.

Allen entered, bowed Buddhist-style to the jury.

Julius looked at Allen as if some strange animal had invaded his home.

For two days Allen turned the courtroom into a religious shrine and filled the courtroom with the most magical vibrations. He brought tears to the eyes of the defendants and kept the spectators breathless. As Allen testified you could have heard a pin drop.

The courtroom was SILENT!

Then came cross-examination, the rigid Catholic Foran going after the free homosexual Ginsberg.

"You consider yourself an intimate friend of Abbie Hoffman and Jerry Rubin?"

"Yes."

"Did you say when you saw Mr. Hoffman on Tuesday night at the Coliseum you kissed him?"

"Yes."

The fear of a man kissing another man rippled through the jury! What degenerates these yippies are!

*The men kiss and fuck each other!*

Then Foran selected some poems for Allen to read. They all concerned cock-sucking, wet dreams, love of man for man.

Homosexuality is the worst sin in Amerika, maybe even worse than Communism.

Allen explained each poem, how we love each other and how our love is repressed in this society. Then Foran sat down, proud of himself—crusader against evil.

Lennie asked Allen to recite *HOWL* and for 20 minutes Allen's massive voice and expressions filled the courtroom and brought us to tears—what a religious moment—what theater; as Allen recited "Moloch, king of power!" he motioned and moved toward Julius, scaring Julie out of his seat.

Allen left the stand to a silent, tearful courtroom.

*"That little fag,"* Foran whispered to Schultz.

A few weeks later Tim Leary was on the stand and he testified how broken I was when Bobby Kennedy was killed because I felt Kennedy was the last hope for Amerika.

I gasped.

Does Leary really believe that? Is communication between Tim and me so bad that he *really* believes *that*? I stopped him and asked him in the defense room at the lunch break.

"No," Tim said, smiling broadly, "but I thought that young juror in the second row liked Kennedy."

Ed Sanders, wearing purple shoes and giving his occupation as a yodeler and peace creep, told how he came to my house for a yippie meeting and for 30 minutes we knelt and prayed before a poster of Che.

Then we ran around the room on Baggies full of ice to get our feet in shape.

*Angela Davis*

The trial was building to a climax, the appearance of Mayor Daley on the stand. When we subpoenaed Daley to testify we all expected he'd move to crush the subpoena.

Daley runs Chicago on a personal kingly basis—and our indictment was the result of his pushing—but the courts like to seem "independent" so Daley stayed behind the curtains. On the last day of the convention demonstrations, Daley's buddy, chief federal prosecutor Tom Foran, empaneled the grand jury to investigate the disorders.

The Attorney General of the USA was opposed to the grand jury but Daley, who felt he and his city had been personally attacked by the rabble, began anyway. Daley and J. Edgar Hoover are old buddies so the FBI began the most extensive investigation since the Warren Commission.

FBI "investigations" are hilarious.

Ostensibly the FBI is to investigate police brutality, as well as demonstrator violence.

But somehow they never quite get around to investigating police violence. That's like asking the police to investigate themselves.

The FBI loved the ass-kicking the Chicago pigs gave to hippies and flippies and dippies.

So the FBI visited everyone. They even went to see Ed Sanders's mother in Kansas!

They travel in pairs, hard cop, soft cop, one FBI agent threatening and warning you about possible indictments and prosecutions, the other smiling warmly and gently saying, "We only want to help you. We are doing this for your own good, you know. If you cooperate with us we will protect you."

The idea is to get you so frightened by Bad Cop that you will rush into the open fatherly arms of Good Cop for help and protection, unaware that they are a team acting out one of Pigdom's oldest routines.

A lot of people do not know that they do not have to speak to the FBI either.

You can shut the door in their face.

You can tell them to go to hell.

You can start reading them the telephone book.

Under no circumstances do you have to speak to them.

Not even if they arrest you!

Tell 'em you'll only speak to them if J. Edgar Freeko comes personally to see you. They cannot make you testify against yourself or your friends. The FBI uses fear and force and people's ignorance of their legal rights to bully or intimidate them into speaking. Nothing you say can help you.

**The FBI is interested only in destroying our movement.**

Then it got closer and we began to see Daley looking over at that jury—after all, they were his people—and saying, "The city felt it was in danger and we did what was necessary to protect the community." He'd melt the hearts of those jurors. Why, it'll probably be the first time any of the jurors have ever seen their mayor—close up! He'd guarantee a guilty verdict.

He'd turn the right-wing jurors into granite against us.

*Daley was no fool.*

We beat him in August '68 in the streets and press, and dealt him the most serious defeat of his political career, but now we were playing in his ballpark, the courts, with his loyal citizens—not the press—judging us. Daley was going to personally throw the weight and prestige of "the city" behind the jury's guilty verdict.

We began to regret the whole thing.

Daley arrived to a loaded courtroom packed with pigs, including his own private bodyguards. He looked like he'd taken 100 downers in the morning. He was as calm as the sea. Buddha himself. He answered questions so softly and quietly—almost a whisper—that we kept having to ask him to speak up.

Julie refused to make Daley an unfriendly witness. "He may have been unfriendly to you as a mayor but he may be friendly to you as a witness," he snapped. Kunstler moved ahead anyway—what a brave motherfucker!

All the questions and objections built up to the climax as Bill asked the most courageous question asked during the whole trial, "Mr. Daley, did you on August 28 say to Senator Ribicoff, **'You dirty Jew bastard sonovabitch— Go home!' "**—at this point Foran was on his feet screaming and yelling and objecting—the jury was excused.

Daley began blushing—" **'You dirty Jew, go home!' "**

Julie flushed.

Bill rushed forward with documents from a lip-reading School of the Deaf to document his question, Julie began scolding him, we were breaking up with laughter at the defense table, Schultz and Foran were shaking their heads in disgust.

The ordeal ended and Daley left the stand. Final tally was 42 questions asked, 38 objections—38 objections sustained. Daley gave his name, his occupation, and that's about all. For his bravery under battle, Kunstler was sentenced to six months in jail.

Our only confrontation took place a few minutes before 2 P.M. after lunchtime when Abbie walked into the courtroom and saw Daley alone on the stand waiting for court to resume. "Hey, Daley, c'mon down here and let's settle this once and for all—me and you. Forget these lawyers and all this legal stuff." Daley smiled.

**"KILL YOUR PARENTS."** Do you mean take a gun and literally shoot them or destroy their way of life and symbolically "kill" them?

*I smile.*

If I said it was symbolic, I'd take all the bite, all the ooomph, all the sex out of the statement.

Few words or statements have the power to shock any more.

When you find one you gotta relish it and take it for all it's worth. Communication is dead. Madison Avenue killed language. Is it literal or symbolic? I don't know myself.

*I guess it depends who your parents are.*

Virtually all political words can be coopted by the PR men in Washington, from "love" to "revolution." When we find one that can't, take it for all it's worth!

Let each kid and every parent decide for him- or herself.

Sometimes the whole thing got so absurd! David Stahl, assistant mayor, testified with a straight face that Abbie offered to call off all the demonstrations for $100,000! Now that was something the city of Chicago could understand!

A bribe!

Extortion!

Finally we yippie leaders were acting in a manner that city officials could relate to.

After all, there had to be something in this for us as individuals. Nobody takes such risks unless they're *on the take*. The people who run Chicago and all the cities of this country are so far apart from our movement in lifestyles and values that the only way *they* can understand *us* is to create us in their image.

The Chicago *Tribune* blazed a six-column black banner page-one headline: **TELL ABBIE'S $100,000 OFFER TO CALL OFF DEMONSTRATION.**

I saw that, and said, now *someone* is crazy.

Them or us.

This world gets battier and loonier every day. Either they're really putting on Chicago citizens or they are whacky themselves. Or maybe we're nuts and everyone else is sane. I began babbling to myself like an idiot and laughing hysterically. Someone might have thought I flipped out.

I did.

How can you remain sane in Amerika without flipping out?

The most fun we had in the courtroom was bringing in our singers. The revolution is poetry—and our generation's poetry is our rock music. Could we get Julie to allow our singers to sing in the courtroom—or would that be behavior unfitting to a courtroom?

First came Phil Ochs, the only one of the singers who was actually brave enough to come to the demonstration. Ochs sang with his throat choked with tear gas. We described the scene in Lincoln Park, and Kunstler asked Ochs what he did next.

As Ochs began to answer we carried in Exhibit 549, Ochs's guitar, and handed it to him while Julie jumped 300 feet in the air. "No singing in *my* courtroom."

The rules of the court were preventing us from recreating for the jury the truthful emotional atmosphere of what went on at the scene of the crime.

We wanted each juror to smoke pot and drop acid to experience our reality.

If we could have tear-gassed the courtroom, we would have, to give the jurors a taste of our reality.

The guitar—a deadly dangerous weapon—was removed from Ochs and not allowed into evidence.

It is a sign of the power of music that it is barred from the courtroom.

Who knows the possible effect on the hearts and souls of the jurors if they had been allowed to hear Phil sing "I Ain't Marching Anymore"? What better way to explain what's going on in the streets!

A few weeks later came Arlo Guthrie. Now Arlo didn't come to Chicago. At the last minute he sorta changed his mind.

We called Arlo to the stand to testify that as evidence of Abbie's and my good faith to put on a music festival in Lincoln Park, we had called on Arlo to come and sing.

And Arlo was to testify that he didn't come because of the bad, bad, violent vibes sent his way by the mayor of the city.

Arlo took the stand and told how he was at radio station WBAI one night and Abbie and Jerry came by and they told me about this festival planned for Chicago and I said groovy, and Abbie suggested that "Alice's Restaurant" be the theme song of the yippies in Chicago and Jerry said he'd never heard the words to "Alice's Restaurant" and I said, "Now it all started two Thanks-givings ago . . . " and as Arlo began to tell the story all the defendants began to giggle because we knew the song was 25 minutes long!

**Arlo gave a shortened version and as he began singing, "You can get anything you want—" Julie rose and shouted, "No singing in *my* courtroom!" and marshals moved toward Arlo and Schultz rose to his feet shouting and we were in stitches again around the defense table and Julie shouted, "If I let you sing, the producers of your movie might sue me!" and Kunstler rushed to the podium shouting, "If that happens, Your Honor, Mr. Weinglass and I will defend you, we'll defend you!"**

Next came Country Joe McDonald. We sat in a restaurant during lunch break dreaming up the afternoon's fantasy.

"Vietnam Rag" would be Joe's contribution to Julie's heart attack and one afternoon's fun and entertainment. But this time we would have to escalate. Could Joe go into a trance and forget where he was? Could he pretend he was in the middle of a be-in, rock festival, dance hall, even in the midst of a shower?

Then everybody—judge, marshals, prosecution—would try to shut Joe up, and he'd think it was part of the show. Joe is a stoned freak and a stoned freak can create his own environment. Bill, Abbie and I started laughing—just in anticipation.

Joe and Julie didn't hit it off too well.

Joe spoke in a slow, quiet acid manner. He was really stoned. He took his time. If everyone had talked as slow as Joe, the trial might have lasted five and a half years. Finally Joe got to that meeting with Abbie and Jerry when Joe told us about this song and suddenly he burst out, " 'Cause it's 1-2-3, What are we fightin' for? . . ."

The courtroom was rent with madness.

You would have thought Joe had pulled out an M-16.

They tried to stop him but Country Joe was in another universe. Finally with Joe screaming and 10 marshals surrounding him and shaking him, Joe stopped.

Joe then stated the words—and the effect was magical.


Judy Collins closed her eyes and the courtroom was suddenly full of "Where Have All the Flowers Gone?" One marshal rushed up to her and physically closed her mouth and held it closed. It was a violent act.

The flowers were crushed.


The question is not whether or not the Washington demonstration is violent. I am not a blood freak. I hate the sight of blood—anybody's blood.

I can't stand to see anyone suffer.

Somewhere in my heart I hold onto the hope that militant and massive nonviolent action can change Amerika. But nonviolence and pacifism are usually cop-outs.

*When the peace marshals sang "Give Peace a Chance," they were in reality singing "Give Nixon a Chance."*

If 20,000 pacifists had clogged the streets in nonviolent resistance, they would have made it more difficult for Nixon to carry out his war.

Pacifists must take the same risks as blacks and poor people or they are using pacifism as a cop-out. Only a white-skinned liberal can afford to be a pacifist.

The oppressor and the liberal cannot tell the oppressed *the means* to free themselves.

Pacifism is a luxury, the exchange one gives for white skin and a privileged place in society.

Dave Dellinger is a pacifist. When the marshals were pushing and pulling and hitting a handcuffed, gagged, shackled and chained Bobby Seale, who do you think was the first defendant to leap out of his seat and come to Bobby's defense? It was the pacifist, Dave Dellinger.

Not the violent revolutionaries among us.

Dave's 200-pound body was in the middle of the action and his elbows were going every direction as he placed his body over Bobby and under the moving arms of the marshals.

"Jesus," I thought, going back to my seat, "I thought Dave Dellinger was a pacifist!"

At the first break I rushed over to Dave and asked him if he still was a pacifist. "Sure," he said, "nonviolence is putting your body in between the attack*er* and the attack*ed.*"

I never had such respect for nonviolence. Or for Dave Dellinger. Unfortunately there is only one Dave Dellinger in the country.

There are probably more pacifists than pigs in Amerika. I got a simple proposal for pacifists.

**Let each pacifist pick out a cop and follow him around eight hours a day, watching everything he does and preaching pacifism to him day and night.**

We gotta turn the country's policemen and professional military men into pacifists. We gotta get the Amerikan soldiers in Vietnam to lay down their arms and start singing "We Shall Overcome" to the Viet Cong. Pacifism can be a powerful tactic eating away at the military morale of this country.

But the pacifists, most of whom are white liberal middle-class intellectuals, have got to start preaching pacifism to the White House, Pentagon and police departments, not to the Panthers and Weatherpeople.

If the appeals court reverses our conviction, and the government is crazy enough to go to trial again, we'll defend ourselves in court. We'll be our own lawyers.

No lawyer, no matter how sincere, can speak with our voice and express our true politics and lifestyle.

Defending yourself humanizes the courtroom. Besides, it will be great fun cross-examining some of those FBI agents.


Three black sergeants came up to our tier to tell us that we had visitors downstairs. I got a funny feeling in my stomach, like a Jew being told, "It's just a shower."

"We don't know what it is, we've just got our orders to bring you downstairs."

"It may be your lawyers, it may be a visit, why don't you just come downstairs and see what it is," one sergeant said, in a smiling, friendly manner.

"No!" we shouted and we rushed back into our tiny jail cells and slammed the doors shut.

We locked ourselves in.

"Leave us in here!"

The guard opened the doors.

"You're not getting haircuts," the sergeant said.

"Yes we are!" we said slamming the jail door locked again.

"Now, c'mon fellows, don't give us a hard time. We're just doing our job," they said as three sergeants jumped me, pulled my arms and handcuffed me behind my back.

Then they ran into Abbie's cell and I heard screaming, and saw a kicking and pushing Abbie led out handcuffed. Abbie, Rennie, Tom and I were then marched downstairs and into a large bullpen next to the barber shop.

"Okay, who's going to be first?" the sergeant said.

"Thought you said you didn't know we were getting haircuts?"

"C'mon, fellas, let's make this easy on everybody."

"We want to speak to the warden!" we said.

"He's not here this morning, fellas."

Tom volunteered to go first and he walked into the barber shop.

Abbie and I sat handcuffed in the bullpen.

They were taking us one by one. After each one went it became that much harder for the next to fight back: dividing us broke our resistance.

"I want to be next," said Abbie.

"If I'm last it'll be too easy."

"Okay, who's next?" said the two sergeants returning.

"Me," said Abbie.

"Let's go, Abbie," they said fatherly.

"No!" Abbie screamed, falling to the floor.

The sergeants picked Abbie up by his hands and feet and began carrying him into the barber shop. The pain around Abbie's hands was excruciating because he was handcuffed and being lifted by hands and feet. They hauled him like a piece of meat and dropped him into the barber shop as Abbie began crying and screaming.

The barber, a black inmate, freaked out and refused to cut the hair of a crying and handcuffed prisoner.

**The sergeant ordered him to cut Abbie's hair, then grabbed Abbie and ordered him to stop crying.**

Abbie by now had begun kicking. Three sergeants pulled his hands against the cuffs and held him down while the barber began to shear Abbie's hair off.

It was a sad and heroic moment. The sergeants really didn't want to do it; the barber was acting under orders; Abbie was resisting.

In the middle of it all Abbie screamed out, "You're ruining my Hollywood career!"

Then they came and got me and pulled me into the barber's chair where the barber whispered into my ear, "I'll first wet it down and I won't cut much off."

"Can we take your handcuffs off, Jerry?" asked the sergeant.

"Will you behave?"

I growled.

They got the message and stood back. "Cutting our hair is like taking off your black skin!" I barked to one sergeant.

"Jerry, I wish you could," he answered. *You don't know how much trouble my black skin has given me.*

What contempt the black bourgeoisie hold for us white hairy niggers! They have fought so hard to become an equal in the white man's society and we are trying to give up our white skin to become a nigger.

We don't appreciate what they want so much.

The barber made good on his whispered promise and left much of the hair on my head.

Sheared, humiliated, beaten—yet still proud of ourselves for resisting—the four of us were then led—surprise!—into the jail photographer's room for new mug shots.

"They'll probably be on the front page of the Chicago *Tribune* today," we cracked, angrily.

We sat down for our shots and each of us tried to look as awful as possible, trying to make our eyeballs disappear from our eyes. At this point the deputy warden entered the room, smiled, pleased at what he saw.

Operation Haircut on the Chicago 7 was successful.

"The pictures will be on page one, won't they?" we asked the deputy warden.

"No, they won't," he said.

"The jail's rules do not allow mug shots to be given to the press. You can be sure of that," he said.

"Sure," we said.

Lying to a prisoner is not really lying.

That night our mug shots were on all three national TV shows and on page one of every Chicago paper—with before and after pictures—and in papers across the country. Three hours later Joe Woods, sheriff of Cook County running for re-election, spoke at a Republican Elks Club and personally displayed his own copy of our mug shots to a cheering and foot-stomping crowd of sterile Republican businessmen.

"Now we Republicans get things done!" Woods said.

Woods told the press that he personally ordered the haircuts.

"All the conspirators willingly got haircuts, no trouble," jail officials were quoted in the press.

"Now Jerry Rubin looks like a nice clean-cut Amerikan boy."

All of our hair was collected from the floor of the barber shop under orders of Sheriff Woods, placed by name in little packages and auctioned off at upper-class Republican fund-raising parties—trophies of the shorn hair of the Chicago 7!

What a strange culture, Amerikan society, collectors of yippie hair and Viet Cong eyeballs.

**Wednesday, July 22**

Our trial was different.
It was a TV trial, a national media trial.
Everyone had to deal with its injustice.
Our hope was that by spotlighting our trial and the injustices of the court system we might call attention to all judges, all trials, all justice—and then by going to jail we might focus the attention of the world on all the poor people held in jail.

The liberals sought a cop-out by focusing on the peculiar personality of Julius Hoffman. We wore buttons saying, "If you've seen one judge, you seen them all," under a Jules Feiffer sketch of Julie.

The right wing had no problem, however.
To them Julie was Every Judge.

Our Conspiracy office in Chicago was a shambles.

Since most of the office staff were women, and all the Conspiracy defendants men, it was a shitty situation—for the men but especially for the women.

*We were on trial as revolutionaries—while at the same time we were oppressors of our own staff.*

Office workers came and went.

To work for us one had to develop a bureaucratic personality and that meant losing all warmth and humanity.

The shitty morale among the defendants led to shitty morale among the staff.

After a long day in court we were too exhausted to meet or deal humanely with staff. I used to get a headache the minute I entered the Conspiracy office and escape to my apartment to get high as soon as I could.

The media attention we got went to our heads and we acted like prima donnas.

It took the women's liberation movement to force us to realize this and

deal with it.

Cliques, special followings and rumors and grudges and bureaucratic hassles made the office a shitty place to work. Hardly anyone survived without their personality being warped and bureaucratized.

At the same time yippellas hung around the office.

**A yippella is a very young yippie who thinks *all* meetings, offices and work is bourgeois and who rebels against the movement like they rebel against their parents.**

A lot of these people are winding up strung out on smack because they haven't found anything to identify with and love.

**If the staff had organized, they might have *forced* the defendants and lawyers to deal with them as equals.**

Since it began, the movement has worked on exploited labor—the labor of women.

Men are crippled in our society because we are trained to think physical chores are beneath us, women do the housework and the office work.

Women at the same time are trained by their parents to accept their lowly status.

The movement must learn to deal with shit work. We are not going to overthrow the government without doing a mountain of shit work.

We cannot do it the way the society we oppose does it—through the promise of money or through force.

Yippellas are wrong in thinking that freedom means no one has to do any shit work.

To defend ourselves against repression and to create a free society we are going to have to do a lot of boring work.

Offices are necessary.

Offices are information and energy centers.

We have to create offices—without bureaucrats and "shit workers." If our movement becomes bureaucratic, its life will be cut off.

Bureaucrats de-organize people.

Can we do all the office work and still be stoned all day?

Can office workers maintain their stoned quality and not become bureaucrats?

The new society will be the institutions and values we create as guerrillas. The new society will be the revolution that makes it.

We have no mechanical program or blueprint—but how we relate to one another will be the revolution we will make, and the society we will create.

**Our daily way of life is our program.**


Women's liberation sprung up partly because veteran movement women had babies and discovered that they were prisoners to their babies, homes and kitchens while their men were still running around as free spirits giving speeches and fucking any women they could.

The sickness of the Amerikan family was repeated in the movement even though the politics were different.

In addition the sexual competitiveness of Amerikan society had women competing against *each other* for men.

Women hated other women. They all made themselves acceptable to macho men.

Finally the pressure broke!

Women began to realize that they had more in common with other oppressed women than they did with their own "men" who did not experience or share their problems. Women began to talk with other women.

Gain self-confidence from each other.

Marriages were broken. Monogamy died.

Men were deserted. Organizations fell apart.

Men were attacked for their sense of humor, much like Amerikan humor in general—jokes about sex from the male point of view: "Women" jokes became as reprehensible to women as "nigger" jokes were to black people.

Men could no longer make jokes about "pieces of ass" or "cunt" or discuss the women they conquered.

Men felt a void in their lives.

Women banded together in revolutionary circles of liberation. And movement organizations fell apart because they were based on women who did all the housework.

Men got frightened because they found themselves more dependent on women than women were on them! Men were the weaker, more fragile sex, less able to survive by themselves.

Women began to pursue issues like the need for the collective caring of children and thereby confronted the crucial life issues of the family, child care, mother-father relations, in a revolutionary manner. The nuclear family is an oppressive institution and we must free ourselves from the family.

A revolutionary confronts the basic problem of society: fear and loneliness.

The revolution must deal with all problems, not just economic and political problems.

Women's liberation will save the movement, forcing men and women to recreate their relationships on a more human basis.

Women and men feel lonely if they don't have an exclusive "mate."

Bourgeois relationships hurt everyone.

*We have to create collectives of lovers.*

The goal of the revolution is to create a classless society, and a classless society is one in which all physical and mental work is shared. The liberation of women as the class of shit workers in the movement is the merging of physical and mental work for all of us.

The media became our organizer. We kept in contact with millions of young people across the country through CBS, ABC, NBC. We lacked local organizers.

Every weekend and many week nights we'd fly all over the USA to speak to overwhelming crowds, where the mere mention of Julius Hoffman's name would reward us with a standing ovation, but that was still relating to people as speaker to mass audience.

We'd fly into a city, drive to the campus, speak for one and a half hours, drive back to the airport and fly out.

Left behind were thousands of turned-on people. The trial had touched a nerve center throughout the nation. Size of the crowds were as great in Wyoming and Utah as they were in Chicago itself. It was a national event.

But how to organize end-of-trial demonstrations?

How could we select a date?

We had no clear idea when the trial would end.

*We wanted our jury to move into the streets as soon as their jury moved into the jury room.*

A lot of people in the movement put down national demonstrations and events 'cause they hamper local organizing when in reality it is national issues and actions which pump adrenalin into local areas.

Every local area is buried in its own pessimism. Wherever go you, the local organizers greet you with the same sad story, "It's awful here, the movement's in terrible shape, everybody's fighting, the pigs are really everywhere." Then two weeks later the place usually blows up.

Every national event, from the Pentagon to the convention week demonstrations to the national college strike after Cambodia, transforms every local area. What seems impossible when looked at from a local perspective becomes natural as part of a nationwide explosion.

Our country is a series of falling dominoes: when one area falls, another falls and then another.

Now there is a freak scene in every city and town and village of Amerika—young kids no longer have to run away to New York or California, all they gotta do is go right down the block.

In 1969 and '70 what had been slowly generating struck the headlines and touched everyone's consciousness, millions of young Southern white freaks!

500,000 at a rock festival in Georgia, more than Woodstock—U. of Alabama torn by bombings, sabotage, demonstrations and hair. In Arizona thousands of yippies have arrived from another planet to frighten the straight citizens of Phoenix and Tucson. I spoke at the U. of Utah to 3,000 freaks who stomped their feet and brought the house down when I suggested that the Mormon Church be destroyed 'cause it oppresses blacks and women.

And Hawaii! That military resort island of US Imperialism is no longer safe for Amerika. Dave and I were out there when students took over the ROTC building and converted it into a living commune.

The media suppresses the story of local wars and it takes a right-wing Senate investigating committee to reveal that 4000 bombings have taken place in the USA in the past 12 months, more than four a day.

The media is determined to no longer romanticize movement violence— instead, the media plays up peace and nonviolence. *To make public is to romanticize.*

When four whites were gunned down in Kent State that was national news and became a national "tragedy"; soon the killing of young whites will no longer even be news. The racist media forgot the murders in Augusta and

Greenville just as soon as they happened while crying for days over Kent State.

The fickleness and fear of the chickenshit mass media forces us to rely on ourselves alone: we must strengthen the underground press and other media things like underground radio 'cause soon you will be able to find out what's happening only in our media.

## Thursday, July 23

The power of our movement is that it is national. We can be isolated and smashed in any local area but if it spreads nationally, we can overextend the government; and if it goes on locally, nationally and internationally, we can win.

**We must transform every local struggle into a national struggle, every local trial—and by now every area has its own version of a Conspiracy Trial—into a national trial.**

Everything is national. Our enemy is national—we must be too. We need powerful local movements with national and international antennae.

*Someday soon we will coordinate demonstrations in every far-out local area of the country with a Viet Cong offensive and with anarchy in Europe and actions by guerrilla movements throughout Latin Amerika, Asia and Africa.*

What happens in Madison, Wisconsin, and New Orleans, Louisiana, is related to what goes on in Bolivia and Laos.

*Every local street is a worldwide battleground.*

A year's growth can take place in a week; a generation is a couple of months; history escalates every day.

Things change so fast I can no longer conceptualize more than a day or a week at a time.

**A month feels like eternity.**

**A year is nowhere.**

**A day is a lifetime.**

**History changes by the minute.**

**Amerika revolutionizes its white youth by putting us in jail. We begin to** *hate the system* **that oppresses people—and** *love the people* **who are oppressed.** Hate and love are both necessary qualities in a revolutionary. Some people don't love the oppressed people enough to be a revolutionary.

The revolutionary is not a suspicious person. Cynicism is a foreign trait.

A revolutionary's soul is made of flowers.

We are so stoned on the future that we cannot believe people are bad. We

212

take people at their word, at face value. And that's why it's been so damn easy for the pigs to infiltrate us.

We don't even like to ask each other's backgrounds because being a revolutionary means you have broken with your past and begun to live life anew. Revolutionaries are reborn souls.

In B.C, Before Chicago, everything was open. We had no secret plans or secret meetings. There were no secret military collectives or small groups operating.

Bob Pierson, a Chicago pig, was accepted as my bodyguard over a mere handshake and embrace and he ran with the "head leaders" of the yippies for a few days and nights.

Irv Bach, a Chicago pig, posed as a Vietnam veteran against the war and within a week was admitted into "secret" meetings, put in charge of self-defense and marshals, and given a lot of office responsibility. No one followed him home to his other existence as suburban family man with two kids and secret police contacts.

Neither Pierson nor Bach got the message—that the movement is always open to strangers, its activities are public and nonconspiratorial, that we have nothing to hide. Instead, Pierson and Bach had to invent a movement full of secret meetings and conspiratorial plans. That's what their superiors expected them to see, and since both were veterans of American military and police structures, they expected the movement to be a left-wing carbon copy of the military and police, with generals, sergeants and lieutenants; public plans and then the real, secret private plans; classified information; exclusive meetings.

Every conversation between me and people in the streets was seen by Pierson as a conversation of a superior to a subordinate.

So when I said to Pierson one morning in an offhand way, **"It's amazing with all the violence here that no one kills a cop,"** it was turned by Pierson on the witness stand to, **"We should isolate and kill a cop."** For two days my gang and I walked the streets and parks of Chicago with Pierson—disguised as a motorcycle gang member with helmet—and not once did the hundreds of people I talked with raise some question or doubts about who this stranger was . . .

### Saturday, July 25

They figured, if he was with us he must be Okay. I figured that since no one else raised questions about him, he must be Okay. **We are so fucking naïve! We want to believe so badly!**

One night I sat in a restaurant with Pierson and three friends when a TV reporter came up to me to say that he'd heard the police had an informer with the yippies. I never suspected Pierson, then sitting right next to me!

A few minutes later Pierson got up to make a phone call. I said to Stew, "Who is this guy?" My immediate fear was that he might be a right-wing assassin posing as my "bodyguard." Stew said, "Jerry, he's socialist man. He's a working-class kid turned on to the revolution by hatred of the pigs. You don't have to read Marx to be a revolutionary." I felt reassured again.

In Chicago during the demonstration we believed our own myth!—that the bikers would join the yippies against the cops. And some bikers really did. But being unfamiliar with the bike culture, we couldn't detect a phony like Pierson and we can't be completely to blame 'cause Pierson came to us after infiltrating a bike gang.

When I was arrested Wednesday night and the pigs brought Pierson—then clean-shaven and dressed in a blue suit—to confront me, I instantly knew he was a pig all along. Thinking back on the week, it was obvious he was a pig.

He was very macho, but we weren't sensitive to macho as a pig trait then.

Also the movement worked on the macho trait of the more militant, the better. Pierson was very militant, suggesting we hold Lincoln Park, tie up Loop traffic, start fires. I dug his militancy. This fallacy of "the more militant, the more revolutionary" has enabled a lot of violent cops to infiltrate the movement with plans of bombing and murder.

You don't suspect them as pigs 'cause a pig never does that, so you go along with it. Then the pigs bust you for the act. Entrapment by a pig is impossible for you to prove. Beware macho. Beware false images of manhood.

Sabotage and bombing are respectable revolutionary acts, but we must be sure who suggests them. We should never, never get involved in any illegal act—or discussions or suggestions of such—with any but our closest friends.

Now I assume that anyone I just meet who suggests we blow up City Hall or kill a cop is a cop.

If you're into bombing why not wear a straight disguise and do a straight trip in your other life?

Never discuss your "victories" with anyone. Most bombers get caught because of their own macho and ego. I suspect that anyone who talks to me about blowing up buildings or killing pigs is a fool—and a liar.

*Those who do, never talk about it.*

*Those who talk about it, don't do it.*

A bomber must have a particular personality. She cannot get ego points for her act. He must be incredibly self-motivated. She is the strongest force in our movement, beyond ego. He will be impossible to infiltrate.

Sometimes you have to choose between open revolutionary activity and underground activity. Different styles are required, although the overground serves and protects the underground. The bomber lives by her example. Those involved in the most violent acts can least afford macho. *Bragging is counter-revolutionary.*

We are going to have to learn to really trust only our closest and longest friends.

Since we are enemies of the state, we express love to each other by being suspicious and careful. We are too illegal to be lax. And when one of us is lax, he or she endangers the lives of others. Our fates are intertwined so suspicion must become a communal responsibility.

We knew pigs could memorize a lot of ideological crap and mechanically rap revolution.

But no pig would grow his hair long.

No pig would smoke dope and maintain his cover.

No pig could run with the outrageous antics of the street theater yippies and Crazies. Then came George Demmerle, and we all learned some important security lessons as well as suffering some horrible blows to our collective cultural egos.

George was the craziest cat around. If you wanted anything flippy done, call George. He lived on the streets and worked with the people. He never took off his yippie button. When the Crazies were born, in an attempt to get an identity distinct from yippie, George nicknamed himself "Prince Crazy, Son of Yippie."

One day George said he had something very important to talk to me about. I put him off because even though I respected George I didn't like him, but I couldn't put my finger on it. I blamed myself, thinking I was some kind of elitist or something and maybe George was too lumpen. Finally, to end the nuisance, I invited George over to my house to see what was on his mind.

*George Demmerle, pig*  *Steve Weiner, pig*

He said the revolution had to go beyond street theater into real disruption and he had this groovy plan to blow up the Brooklyn Bridge. I winced. "Well, go do it, George," I said, "and don't talk about it. What do you need me for?"

George left. I thought to myself, "Boy, that Prince Crazy sure is crazy."

During the famous presidential march of Pigasus the pig across New York, George dressed as a classical anarchist bomber with long coat and hat over his head, and made a fierce attempt to grab the pig. Other yippies dressed as

217

plainclothes pigs grabbed George and tossed him head first into the Hudson River! Now what kind of policeman would be so devoted to do a thing like that? That was one of the freakiest guerrilla theater acts ever.

**It's since come out that not only was George a cop but so was one of the "yippie pigs" who heaved him in the water!**

When the New York bombers were finally caught, after frightening the city for weeks with brilliant attacks on key capitalist symbols, setting off thousands of bomb scares and forcing paranoid building after paranoid building to stop its work, empty its inhabitants into the streets and search the premises, a group of bombers was arrested. George was one of them.

I thought to myself, "Yeh, George was crazy enough to do something as brave as that. You got to be a little crazy to be so brave."

**For us calling someone "crazy" is paying them a high compliment.** Then a day later I read that George was released without bail on the prosecution's motion and he was going to testify for the government.

My heart stopped.
I felt so shitty.
George's emergence as an FBI informer for eight years dealt a temporary blow to the freaky movement in New York. The Crazies broke up. A lot of the young kids whom George had recruited into the movement disappeared. Only the most committed could withstand the shock. Remember Prince Crazy and all his funny uniforms? He always came to demonstrations dressed in purple hats and capes. Well, he was a John Birch Society member, and maybe even possibly a Minuteman, who infiltrated the movement and stayed up late every night filing reports for the FBI.

## Sunday, July 26

If an undercover pig believes in his or her act, he can pull it off. If he doubts himself, he'll give himself away. So it's no surprise that it was a right-wing extremist who posed as a left-wing extremist.

A part of George is Prince Crazy or he wouldn't have been able to do it. You got to be a little mentally unbalanced to live so many different lives. You got to be a little crazy. And it is these people who the government counts on for its information and convictions against us. Schizophrenics are the government's main source of information against us.

The goal of undercover pigs like George is to demoralize us and make us so paranoid that we suspect each other and become totally ineffective. It would

be very counterrevolutionary to oppose a military, freaky action by saying that only pigs do militant, freaky things.

Pig-baiting is counterrevolutionary. We should oppose actions on political grounds, not by attacks on the people suggesting them. Paranoia is a movement cancer paralyzing us. Beware of paranoia. Stamp out paranoia.

Some people are so frightened of the pigs that they do nothing. They won't talk on the telephone 'cause the phone is tapped. **By saying your phone is tapped you can do nothing and still consider yourself a militant revolutionary 'cause your phone is tapped.**

By making you *believe* your phone is tapped the government saves expense because then they don't have to tap your phone. They've rendered you useless through psychological warfare.

Just like paranoia is our greatest weapon against them, so paranoia is their greatest weapon against us.

If they succeed in getting us to believe that everyone is a cop and all meetings are bugged and the pig is everywhere, then they do not even have to infiltrate us because they have infiltrated our minds and rendered us absolutely immobile.

Beware the tapped phone and bugged meeting and everyone's a cop complex. Oversecurity is macho; oversecurity is conservatism disguised as militancy.

Their goal is not to bust us—it's too messy to bust all of us—but to paralyze us, render us ineffective, put us on the sidelines. We must never let pig-fear prevent us from doing what we feel is right to do.

The phone probably is bugged but for 95 per cent of the things we do it doesn't make a damned bit of difference whether or not the pig knows it or not. People are now afraid to have even the most casual conversation on the phone.

Just because pigs suggest street theater and sabotage does not mean that street theater and sabotage are wrong. Sometimes pigs have the best ideas.

I always thought the plan—first suggested by a New York pig disguised as a black militant—to blow up the Statue of Liberty was an outasight revolutionary idea.

Often undercover pigs know best what will fuck up the pigs and they suggest such actions to win our confidence.

But we must not underestimate our enemy; soon we will have pigs who aren't macho and we already have women undercover pigs.

We are going to have to learn to live in that dynamic area between overestimating and underestimating our enemy; between naïvete and paranoia; between faith and security. By creating undercover pig paranoia the Pig is trying to create walls between us and the people, forcing us to be suspicious of every new person.

And that is death to a movement that can only survive by growing.

We gotta count on dropouts and the disaffected who join the revolution because we are right and we are winning. Of course by winning over the youth—the children of FBI, CIA, Pentagon chiefs—we are doing the best infiltrating of all.

We got a spy in every one of their homes—their own kids!

**Our intelligence network of children spying on their own fathers puts their pathetic undercover pig system to shame. We beat 'em! We stole their kids!**

We must be as above ground as possible, with open offices, meetings and activities to reach new people.

Going underground too quickly would be like giving up, committing suicide.

We have gotten more tight with each other and that's good. Survival creates interdependence which creates close comradeship. Our lives and futures become One. The survival of each of us affects the other. One fuck-up endangers a lot of other people.

But that does not rule out open, mass organizing with offices and meetings. Open organizing will always be the most important organizing of all. There must always be a public place and phone where new people can go to hook up to the movement and be greeted with open arms.

A lot of our defense was based on convincing the jury of the psychological instability of the undercover pig. While we were doing this in the courtroom by day, we learned later that the marshals were "entertaining" the jury at night with James Bond films.

Middle-class professional whites and blacks, doctors, ministers, businessmen, intellectuals, professors should take advantage of their white skin privilege and directly confront Amerika through massive and continual civil disobedience.

Block the courtrooms.

Throw yourself in front of the *New York Times* trucks.

Block bridges and stop rush-hour traffic of a big city.

Close down Washington. Follow the pigs around and make their lives miserable for them.

Block police stations.

Close down the universities.

The image of Amerika in flames and unable to govern itself is important for young people and oppressed people throughout the world. The intellectual class must break with its style of life and its own notion of respectability and do the extreme, the absurd, the shocking act. No one listens to intellectuals in Amerika unless they act like children and troublemakers.

We must redefine what it means to be "respectable" in Amerika. Through massive arrests white middle-class people can focus public attention on the most repressive institution in Amerika: the courts.

Why have white skin privilege if you're not going to use it for the revolution?

### A RIOT IS A PARTY.
A speech is a public celebration.

We live together on the streets. A speech is not an exchange of information—it is an emotional event with everyone touching each other. It is a revival meeting. We are charged emotionally.

The speaker tries to get the audience to react. A good speaker polarizes, forcing the white racists to expose their racism, the liberals to squirm nervously and the liberated to start dancing.

Right-wing disrupters are vital to any successful yippie freakout. They provide the straw man every good rabble rouser needs.

The good speaker expresses the thoughts and feelings that are on everybody's lips but most people are afraid to say.

At the end of the speech the yippie has converted souls, reinforced the faithful and revamped the power forces on any campus.

The only thing that remains after the speech is to *act*.

The straight student's "mind" and "reason" tells them to be cautious and not to listen but they indulge a little 'cause they are anxious and uncomfortable because their country is falling apart—and maybe this freak is right after all!

They cannot deny the truth once they hear it stated loudly. They are reduced to crying, "But what can *we* do about it?"

And the freaks respond in chorus, "Do It!"

*The freaks are freeing the students.*

*The straights are losing their minds.*

### THE BEST SPEECH IS A BANNED SPEECH.
If they let us speak we bring large crowds together and turn them on. If they ban us a riot is inevitable. Whatever the Establishment does—toleration or repression—it loses.

### Tuesday, July 28

I remember an automobile ride from O'Hare Airport to a hotel where The Conspiracy defendants and lawyers were going to meet for the first time the day before our arraignment. I'll never forget it. I arrived in Chicago by plane from New York about the same time Bobby Seale and Charles Garry arrived from San Francisco, so I waited to get a lift from them into the Loop.

Fred Hampton met Bobby at the airport and on the way in by car we laughed and told stories and discussed the trial.

My attention focused on the driver of the car, Fred Hampton. I was wildly impressed by him, only twenty years old! It was the first time Fred met Bobby. Fred ran down to Bobby the state of the Illinois party, all the beefs on his head, "I got 10 years! For stealing 89 ice cream bars and giving them out free to the kids in the neighborhood!"

Hampton showed that the Black Panthers, started in Oakland, were growing—they were reaching the most powerful youth in the black ghetto. The next day at a rally I saw Fred speak and he electrified the crowd with his energy and passion: "**I AM A REVOLUTIONARY!**" he had the crowd chanting.

Hampton was the kind of leader whose self-confidence and drive would inspire other young blacks to join the party. When I saw him I thought of Huey, Eldridge, Bobby—now Fred Hampton. Isn't there something ominous about Hampton? A cloud of death hung over his head.

He told us how the pigs were after him—"We don't have much time."

*Hampton's body removed by laughing police*

Eight months later:

Bobby Seale, the last Panther leader on the streets without heavy beefs, would be in jail facing the electric chair on a trumped-up conspiracy-to-murder beef and be taken to and from the courtroom in Chicago every day in handcuffs and chains.

Chicago Gestapo would invade Fred Hampton's home, find him sleeping, riddle his body with bullets and kill this young black dynamo—a cold-blooded assassination.

Everything was so happy and so free in that car ride from O'Hare to the Loop. But Hampton was right. "We don't have much time. If they don't jail us they're going to kill us."

Boston's youth community is outasight 'cause of the hitch-hiking way of life.

Thousands of young kids hitch-hike up and down the street, meeting each other, exchanging energy, telling stories, spreading gossip. It's the best way to communicate in the city, driving your car up and down Massachusetts Avenue, picking up people or hitch-hiking up and down the street. The streets become human in the youth community. You go into the streets to see your friends.

*The legal oppression of Bobby Seale is the oppression of the Black Panther Party is the oppression of black people for 400 years.* Bobby Seale is on trial 'cause Bobby Seale is a black revolutionary.

Bobby Seale was not going to accept this attempted destruction of him in a passive or defeated manner. Bobby Seale struck back.

Bobby Seale put the state on trial.

Bobby Seale set an example in the courtroom for everybody being railroaded into jail.

Julius Hoffman refused to postpone the trial for six weeks until Bobby's lawyer, Charles Garry, recovered in the hospital from an operation. So Bobby

was forced into the trial without his lawyer. He decided to represent himself and be his own lawyer.

Bobby studied law books showing the Sixth Amendment and right to "effective" counsel of "your own choice" and one morning he got so excited, practically jumping up and down, when he discovered a Reconstruction law that guaranteed black people equal protection under the law as a result of the Civil War.

*Bobby told me Huey taught him that revolutionaries must know the Man's law better than the Man and use it against him.*

So Bobby held the Constitution and law books in his hand. As the defendants met after court Bobby warned us against disrupting the trial. "There's no need for you guys to get locked up too. You're needed out there speaking and explaining to people what I am doing."

Bobby's eyes gleamed as he talked. They danced. He'd sit back and roar with happiness at the challenge Life offered him. "This is my issue. I'm guaranteed my rights. The Constitution says so." It always amazed us that Bobby expressed such a revolutionary faith in the Constitution.

And then in the middle of our strategy meetings Bobby would go on and on in a monologue to us about his legal rights and the Constitution, forgetting that we didn't need convincing, but so excited about his battle that he couldn't stop rapping. We loved Bobby.

It was rough on him. He knew that every time his name was mentioned he must rise and demand to defend himself.

But the repression was incredible. Before Bobby could have three words out, Julius and the prosecutors would be screaming, the jury would be excused—some of the jurors were so scared of Bobby they'd be running out of the room as he rose—and the marshal would be on top of him.

To continue under that kind of control would take superhuman discipline and struggle. Only the fierce belief that he was right pushed Bobby on.

During the first two weeks of the trial I was in Cook County Jail with Bobby Seale. We'd come to and from court together chained and handcuffed and spend hours together waiting in jail lock-ups. I don't think I ever saw Bobby down once. He was facing the chair on a frame-up in Connecticut yet he was always high, bubbling, rapping about Huey, the party's ten-point program, his dreams, the party's history.

One time in a paddywagon we drove past about 60 young black schoolchildren playing ball. "Isn't it something," Bobby said, "half those kids will be in jail before they are twenty."

One morning he had 30 prisoners in stitches with his mimics of LBJ, John Kennedy, Hubert Humphrey. Bobby was a stand-up comic before he became a Panther. He's an actor: "Oh, if I could only get out of here so I can play Malcolm X in a movie version of his life! Think of all the black kids seeing that movie!"

To Bobby living is experiencing. When he was a kid he used to cut himself on the arm just to see what it felt like. He showed me the scars. "If I go to the electric chair I'll go there—life is experience—and I'l have the experience of that."

For hours we were locked up and Bobby never stopped rapping, stoned on his own energy. Even though there were only two of us in the lock-up, he'd stand and wave his arms and scream and jump as if he were speaking to thousands of people, on things like self-defense, African history, Huey, how black people are a nation. He ran through the history of the party. I wished I had a tape recorder and TV to show to the world.

Not once did Bobby express fear or self-pity. He knew as a revolutionary this was natural, to be in and out of jail. He was busy writing a novel in jail at night about the history of the party.

Hundreds of lawyers told us that Julius's treatment of us in the trial was typical—that's the way he's been railroading defendants, mistreating lawyers and terrorizing people from the bench for years—but it took a ghetto nigger to take Julius on directly, confront him, expose him and defeat him.

Lawyers cowed before Julius but Bobby stood up to him.

And the prosecution and judge played on all the anti-black fears they could. To them every time Bobby rose he had a knife in his hand ready to plunge it into Julius's stomach.

The government brought in specially a 6-foot 6-inch 300-pound black marshal named Preston to stand and guard over Bobby. They filled the courtroom with every black marshal they could find to try and deflate Bobby's plea of racism, and to add absurdity to it all on the day they gagged Bobby they even brought in their only black court stenographer. We half expected Julius to come in blackface!

*Yet Bobby was very nonviolent.* He practically tiptoed around the courtroom. He raised his voice only when Julius tried to scream him out. Bobby was polarizing the courtroom.

The battle escalated one morning when Bobby told Julius, **"If you don't grant me my constitutional rights, then you are a pig."**

"What did you say?" Julius retorted. "You called me—a federal judge—a **PIG?"**

Julie loved to whine about the violence of Bobby calling him a pig. It may be the first time a judge was ever called a pig. Here Bobby was being railroaded to jail for 10 years—and Julius was upset about being called a pig.

The executioner always loves to play the victim.

Sitting above Julius's head were pictures of the Founding Fathers.

"You've even got a picture of a slaveowner, George Washington, hanging right behind you on the wall in this courtroom," Bobby said to Julius.

That made Julie happy—to be compared with George Washington.

And that was even a little too much for us.

We had been pointing out the hypocrisy of Julius getting inspiration from the country's eighteenth-century longhair revolutionary founders while prosecuting twentieth-century longhair revolutionaries.

But it was black Bobby Seale laying bare the fundamental contradiction of Amerika.

*Was George Washington the founder of Bobby Seale's country?*

To Bobby Seale, George Washington was a slaveowner.

We began to see George Washington from the viewpoint of Bobby Seale, not Julius Hoffman.

Bobby was right—George Washington and Julius Hoffman deserved each other.

Bobby was up demanding his rights constantly and Julius could not emotionally handle it. Julius was ready to break. Julius was obviously going to break before Bobby.

As everyone in the courtroom held their breath, Julius ordered the marshals to take Bobby in the backroom "and deal with him as he should be dealt with."

Within minutes Bobby was carried back into a stunned courtroom with his legs and arms handcuffed to a chair and his mouth taped.

Some jurors began weeping.

It was an incredible sight to see Bobby gagged and chained there—it made you sick to your stomach and filled you with raging anger and hate at Julius Hoffman, Tom Foran, Richard Schultz and the US government.

Ten minutes later Bobby broke his arm free, ripped off the gag and began shouting for his constitutional rights.

As Bobby broke free and began speaking out, federal marshals jumped him, knocking him over and into the press section. Other defendants moved to Bobby's aid and defended him in pushing and shoving battles with marshals. The jury was excused and the courtroom was in a shambles.

Julius directed the marshals to do it better. This time they grabbed Bobby's nose, and forced his mouth open and pushed tape down his throat. Then they taped over his head, causing blood to leave Bobby's head and make him faint.

They carried Bobby back into the courtroom as Julie kept insisting, "I'm the best friend, Mr. Seale, your people have ever had. I'm doing this for your own good—to guarantee you a fair trial."

Minutes later Bobby moistened the gag and began making clear sounds.

The beautiful music from Bobby Seale's body stopped the courtroom.
**It was impossible to gag Bobby Seale.**
**It was impossible to silence Bobby Seale.**

During his daily battle with Julius Hoffman Bobby asked the seven white defendants not to disrupt the trial. He didn't want to take the issue off his constitutional right for legal self-defense, and widen it into a general issue of courtroom disruption.

But when Julie escalated by finally sentencing Bobby to four years for contempt of court and cut him from the case, we other defendants should have become really disruptive, throwing chairs and tables around, forcing Hoffman to gag and chain us all or stop the trial.

That would have been a powerful visual demonstration of black-white revolutionary unity, and might have set off a chain reaction across the campuses and ghettos of Amerika.

But our meetings ended up in collective indecision and fear. We could not unite.

What we did do was spontaneous and powerful, and our support for Bobby was strong. We ended up getting years in jail for our actions in support of Bobby during the gagging.

It is wrong to put *all* the responsibility on the other seven defendants and ask why we didn't do more. Anything we would have done would have ended up in a long automatic jail sentence without bail and therefore seemed suicidal. We felt we could do more by continuing the trial and exposing the court system.

What was more disturbing was the silence of *all* young people throughout Amerika.

No one did anything when Bobby was gagged or Fred was killed—making the pigs feel they can do anything to blacks, and young whites will accept it.

Until that gap between the black and white revolution is bridged, no true alliance can really be built.

Bobby was creating a theater in the courtroom that exposed the soul of Amerika for everyone to see. His victory inspired prisoners in courts and jails throughout Amerika.

All black people are gagged and chained in Amerika's courtrooms. But because the gags and chains are invisible, we cannot see or experience them.

Bobby Seale forced us to see and experience them directly.

The shackling was Bobby's triumph, not his defeat.

**JULIUS HOFFMAN HAD VIOLENT STATE POWER ON HIS SIDE— THE MARSHALS AND THE JAILS—BUT BOBBY SEALE HAD THE TRUTH AND SOUL OF HUMANITY ON HIS.**

The first and second generation of New Lefters in their late twenties and early thirties who have remained "straight radicals" are as vital to the movement as all those old men and women in their forties and fifties who keep fighting over and over again yesterday's Communist Party or labor struggles.

The movement must be protected against yesterday's leaders.

Every new struggle pushes new leaders forward. There is no more New Left. It is Old and Dead.

The study of history forces us to repeat it. We are now the youth, the youth culture. Terms of "left" and "right" are too confining.

We are now all young people; we are *the future*.

The first generation of radicals was born in the graduate schools and their radicalism was an extension of their brain. Generations now are born at the be-ins, riots, rock dances and dope parties. We are no longer an intellectual fringe elite minority; we are now the freaky youth masses.

And isn't it odd—the intellectuals who forever croon about reaching the working class can't do it because of their intellectual class snobbery; young middle-class kids are now relating to the children of workers through music, dope and action in the streets.

We need national coordinating centers, information centers, to keep local areas in contact with each other; to help create national Communist economic institutions; to produce buttons and posters and national symbols; to wage a coordinated attack against psychedelic capitalism like the movie *Woodstock*; to create a place where organizers can communicate; to take the energy of yippie and turn it into organization power; to organize national demonstrations and pow-wows; to represent the party and nation in relations with the Panthers, Cubans and Viet Cong; to communicate directly by phone and letter with the millions of young kids still held prisoner in their homes, schools, jails and mental institutions; to spread the myth; to fight hard dope; to build liberated communities; to publish a national underground paper.

When yippie was created in December, 1967, it was hatched as a myth, war cry and organization, the Youth International Party. Some day, we dreamed, the myth will grow and grow until there will be millions of yippies and they will create a loosely organized party.

In 1970 yippies were everywhere. YIP is a loose confederation of the Crazies. Soon there will be yippies and a Youth International Party throughout the Western world.

Yippie changes as reality changes.

*Yippie in the summer of 1970 was taken over by yippie women who confronted directly the male chauvinism of hippie-yippie culture.*

Women took over national yippie mythmaking, with yippies Nancy Kurshan and Judy Gumbo and White Panther sister Genie Plamondon going on a trip to North Vietnam and working on a proposed trip of yippies to meet the North Vietnamese in Cuba.

Yippie groups appeared all over the country with women and men working together and struggling together. Gay yippies came out, and Gay YIP groups began.

Yippie includes women and men, gays and straights. Women organizing as women and gays as gays is good but it is only on one level—on another level we should be working and struggling together, women and men, gays and straights, to create new sexual patterns, new relationships, new values.

Somewhere between the superdiscipline structure of the White Panthers and the chaos of the yippies we must find a balance, not in theory but in practice. To survive we will have to get together.

Yippies should create a loosely organized mass youth movement. We must try to make the revolution as free, open and as yippie as possible. Our organization should be bottom up, not top down. Leadership by example. Faction fights dissipate and drain energy.

*Our organization should be based on communes and collectives.*

YIP must put Abbie and me in our place. Our role as celebrities and national figures forces us into a maddening lifestyle of hopping from city to city often traveling by airplane along with business people and rock groups.

When we arrive on a campus the power of our myth enables us to bring people together. It is not by accident that riots usually follow our appearances within a month although we do not incite or organize them.

Our myth is greater than we are.

But our power must be put at the service of YIP both for the good of the revolution and for our own survival and health.

Our celebrity status demands more ego satisfaction to fit its own expectations, like a fix. We must fight our own individualism and egoism and live collectively.

Hopefully within YIP, pacifists, White Panthers and Weatherpeople will work together. In a revolution there should be no conflict between militant nonviolence and armed struggle; the most effective will prove itself morally and politically right. The violent revolutionaries will be successful only if they are fish in the sea. This will guide their choice of tactics and should make them morally acceptable to the pacifists.

The Weatherman were ideologically fucked up at first when they saw themselves as a violent Viet Cong minority behind enemy lines out to inflict material physical damage against Imperialism. At this stage of the movement, the amount of damage we can inflict is minimal indeed.

**Our power is our ability to light a fire among the youth and create widespread national disruption.**

Bernardine Dohrn's "New Morning" statement showed that Weatherpeople have extended their tactics from pure military damage to mass organizing of freaks. We are not going to organize the people around our ability to suffer. We are going to organize the people around our ability to have fun and to survive.

Some people relate in a fucked-up way to the Weatherpeople. Revolution becomes a spectator sport, with folks sitting back and wondering what the Weatherpeople are going to blow up next. The Weatherpeople become super heroes, athletes and myths, out of reach of the people.

*Yesterday's activist becomes today's "right-on-er!"*

Saying "right on!" is about all some people do. We become fans at an athletic match, rooting for the Weatherpeople versus the Pigs. That is fucked up. That will endanger the safety of the Weatherpeople.

They can survive only if we create a mighty sea to swim in. What is so beautiful about the Weatherpeople is that they are people like us, our friends, our close friends, our sisters and brothers, who have taken on new identities and are living in the USA as fugitives, creating an underground network.

We must not pressure them by saying: "The Weatherpeople haven't blown up anything recently. They must have dropped out."

For the Weatherpeople to survive and keep organizing is a massive victory for the revolution. It is a total defeat for the pigs.

*Every hour we should be calling the FBI in our local city and telling them we just saw Bernardine Dohrn and here's where she is!*

Bomb threats are a mass movement.

Anybody can do it.

All you need is a dime.

If the USA bombs North Vietnam again, we can shut down every major airport in the USA with a lot of phone calls.

The Weatherpeople have brought a realness to the revolution with bombs. When the underground blows up a draft board it is the logical extension of the liberals writing to their congressmen to end the war. Everything else takes on more importance now that the left is into dynamite.

The bomb that went off at Centre Street, the New York Police Station headquarters, shows that no place is safe for the pigs.

We are everywhere.

Four thousand bombs went off in the USA last year by the left. But we are not going to blow Amerika up pig building by pig building. That's impossible. The goal of armed struggle now is to raise the consciousness of the people.

An army without the consciousness of the people cannot win.

*Symbols win the support of the people; symbolic victories give everyone a high.*

A role for the revolutionary today is to be provocateur, provoking large-scale revolutionary confrontations between the state and masses of people. Revolutionary action is mass action, involving the *largest* number of people.

The best mass action is spontaneous, flowing from the people. "Leaders" and "vanguards" hold back the energy and anger of the people.

If bombers think the only thing to do is bomb, they will be isolated. We must not look at the movement in a linear way. We go from lower stages to higher stages but that does not mean we abandon the lower stages.

The movement must do all things simultaneously.

Pacifism eats at the morale of the army while we bring guerrilla war to the cities.

Pacifism and sabotage go hand in hand. Those who excel in one field should not put down those who excel in another. The movement operates on all levels eating away at the cancerous structure of Amerika.

What distinguishes a revolutionary act is confrontation; we are never at peaceful coexistence with Amerika, wherever we are we are always confronting and polarizing. The goal of the revolutionary saboteur is to bomb and then convince the liberal to defend his or her act.

Violence must be symbolic and gain the support of the "nonviolent" masses.

*Bombing buildings without killing people is an example of revolutionary violence.*

Killing people would be counterrevolutionary. Killing people accidentally in bombings is counterrevolutionary.

Only in the most extreme and symbolic case or in self-defense should we even consider killing a pig. There will always be another pig to take his place. However, it would have been a revolutionary act to assassinate Hitler in 1939.

Bombers must gauge their tactics with the struggle and consciousness of all youth.

Revolution morality demands that you attack in defense, not offense—at this stage of the people's consciousness.

Macho violence is a great threat to the future of the movement.

So is do-nothing pacifism.

Confrontational pacifism and symbolic revolutionary violence are our revolutionary tactics.

Meanwhile key areas of the country were preparing for the demonstrations when the trial ended. Boston came up with the mythic concept: a simple blue button with three letters, TDA. When I wore it into court Foran asked me what it meant. "The Day After," I said. Foran got the message.

234

Our troops were mobilizing. TDA buttons swept the country. Then, as usual, Julius did the impossible. He shocked us all. All our lawyers and all the wags around the Federal Building said Julius would never sentence us to jail before the jury verdict. It would look like Julius had no respect for the verdict of the jury.

Whenever we tried to predict what Julius or the government would do we were always wrong.

*What Julius did was always more awful, cruel and oppressive than we ever imagined.*

The jury door was not closed a second before Julius said, "Now it is my responsibility to deal with the disruption . . . "

Sadism is very greedy.

Dave was first and Julius kept reading all of Dave's contempts. We each kept notes, like keeping score. Hearing Julius read Dave's lines made them sound so convincing. We felt like shouting **RIGHT ON**!

Julius finished reading and gave Dave a chance—finally!—to speak on his own behalf. Dave's body was shaking and his voice quivering.

Marshals moved on Tasha and began pulling and pushing her in an effort to remove her from the courtroom for spontaneously applauding her own father's final statement before he was going to jail for a long time.

Dave started screaming, helplessly, "Leave my daugher alone! Leave my daughter alone!" All over the room spectators were shouting at the marshals as more and more marshals piled into the courtroom.

Tasha was kicking. Fights broke out elsewhere. Chairs fell over. The marshals were clearing the room of the "rabble."

It was the complete breakdown of the judicial process.

Bill broke down at the violence. Tears began streaming down his eyes. He fell to his hands and knees before the judge and said, "Your Honor, look what you have done. You've destroyed all I believe. Take me now, please. Take me now."

All of a sudden I found myself jumping to my feet up and down like a jack in the box, my feet goose-stepping and my right hand high in the air. "Heil Hitler! Heil Hitler!" I shouted. "That's how you should be greeted. Heil Hilter!" The room was full of "Heil Hitler!" as the marshals removed Dave's daughter and forced truce upon the room. Julie sentenced Dave to four years. We were being hung one by one. Then came Rennie. Boom! 23 months, one year of which when Rennie was on the witness stand.

Julius hit Hayden hard, 14 months contempt.

Then came Abbie. Julius sentenced Abbie to eight months.

Then came my turn and Julius did the cruelest thing of all. He canceled court until morning.

"No, sentence me now," I shouted. Julius snapped back, "Would you ask a favor of Adolf Hitler?" What an eerie feeling being free for my last night, knowing that tomorrow morning I'd be locked up. We hung around the courtroom for a while. Reporters took bets on how much contempt I'd get. I worked on my statement. I got stoned. Nancy and I spent our last night together. I had an awful cold and I buried the symptoms with codeine.

I got 24 months. Froines got six months and Lee two and then Julie smacked his lips, licked his chops, and got ready for his pièce de résistance— Bill Kunstler. That upstart lawyer who dared to represent such vermin, who dared to talk back to me, Julius Hoffman. Bill got four years and Lennie two.

So there we were all in jail. It seemed like a fitting ending to a sadistic play marked with tragedy and humor.

We felt like pinching ourselves to see if it were true. Making history is like living a dream. We got finger-printed three times. We were given numbers and armbands. Our possessions were removed. We stripped three different times and guards looked up our ass, through our long hair and in our mouths to see if we were smuggling any dope or guns in. We had to sit on wooden benches for six hours waiting to get processed. We were offered contaminated baloney on stale white bread. Our blood samples were taken. We filled out questionnaires giving names of kin in case of injury or death while in jail.

Then we were led up to the tier where troublemakers, political organizers, homosexuals, jailhouse brawlers, high-security prisoners, cop-killers are kept on double lock. We were fed dinner when the guard shoved food under our door. Tom and I were in the same cell. Remember the jury? We almost forgot!

We asked a guard, "What time is it?" and he barked back, "What do you care? You going somewhere?"

Kunstler was being blamed for inciting the burning of the Bank of America at Santa Barbara. Berkeley and San Francisco pig stations were blown up and two cops killed. *The trial certainly had not proved a deterrent to stop riots.*

When we heard the bank was burning, we knew we would soon be free! We also knew that the struggle had moved to a higher stage. A mass youth movement had protested our trial not by holding a teach-in but by burning a bank.

The riots broke out spontaneously and anarchistically across the country and the office became an inspiration center. Nancy and Anita dramatically poured gasoline over judge's robes outside the Federal Building under a sign saying, "We Are All Outlaws in Eyes of Amerika."

In three days the women in the office organized the largest Conspiracy demonstration in Chicago—a mass march of 10,000 from the Federal Building to the county jail.

Mafia leaders in Cook County Jail told us we'd never get appeal bond—the case was too hot.

One Saturday morning two weeks after going to jail, we were rapping with our once-a-week visitors when a bulletin hit the radio: The appeals court set a bond.

We were freed but we were sad.

We were sad because of all the people we had left behind us in jail.

**Never again would we ever enjoy ourselves—whether it's getting stoned, enjoying good food, being with friends—without being aware at the same time of all the human beings that are at that second locked up behind bars in Amerika.**

A week later we got $15,000 together and Rennie returned to our tier to bail out 20 prisoners who were in jail 'cause they couldn't afford their own bonds—a small, token gesture but an important move. It did not satisfy our consciences but it was a move in the right direction—a move the movement should take as it begins to serve the people.

Getting on the streets was the weirdest feeling. Wherever we went, friends, acquaintances and strangers embraced, hugged and kissed us and said, "Oh, I'm so happy you're not in jail."

Freeing us was a concrete victory for our movement because young people did it by their actions in the streets. If it weren't for those actions, we'd still be in jail, forgotten lumps of human meat stored in animal boxes.

Wherever we went we were loved. It was the ecstasy of our movement felt during peak moments of our struggle when everyone is together, all grudges, differences, personal antagonisms and ego fights are forgotten and we all touch each other with love.

We were martyrs and we weren't even dead!

*Being an alive martyr is some trip!*

Soon the halo over our heads would be gone and we'd be the victims like everyone else of rumors, personality fights and faction struggles.

Our movement eats itself up with criticism.

No "leader" should be treated differently than anyone else.

But wouldn't it be wonderful if all treated each other *all the time* the way we treat each other during peaks of battle?

So the martyrdom would be short-lived.

The attacks and the suspicious glances would soon begin.

It was a rough year.

A year of Fear.

Fear in jail and Fear in the courtroom.

But we must recognize our fear and overcome it. We are not Superwomen and Supermen.

We are human beings trying to be revolutionaries, and we must constantly struggle to rise above our limitations and be stronger women and men.

Every day we are becoming stronger and more loving revolutionaries.

I fell in love with Charlie Manson the first time I saw his cherub face and sparkling eyes on national TV. When I was out in L.A. on a speaking gig Manson saw me on TV giving a rap, and asked his lawyers to find me and bring me to see him in jail.

I heard about it and Phil Ochs and I went to L.A. city jail to meet Charlie's three lawyers.

We met Gypsy and Squeaky, two of the Manson Family not in jail, and they were outasight. Squeaky is tiny with a squeaky voice, blond hair, blue eyes and a face and smile you'd trust. She's supposed to have offed a couple of people but I don't believe it. Squeaky? No!

She told me she was once a married secretary working in San Francisco who took a walk through Haight-Ashbury, met Charlie by accident and never returned to her job or husband.

The lawyers arrived and told the pigs that Phil and I were material witnesses in the case. I had no identification but that didn't seem to be any problem and we were lightly searched and whisked into the jail.

Through the window we saw Charlie: his beard was gone. We exchanged clenched fists.

We were led to a glass-enclosed room with a table and five chairs. Someone had snuck a tape recorder under his jacket and was going to tape the meeting.

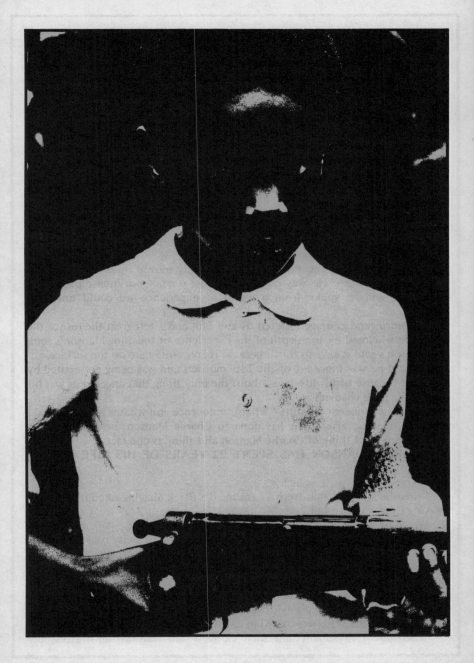

Charlie entered. I tried to shake hands or embrace. "No, you can't touch me," said Charlie, wise to the ways of prison.

"Do you mind if I rap?" Charlie asked. We said no and Charlie began a three-hour rap, rarely taking his hypnotic eyes off us, and only stopping for a question or comment from us.

I felt myself getting hypnotized by his penetrating eyes. Charlie's face showed the suffering of years behind bars. You could tell from his face that this guy had been through a lot.

*"Rubin, I am not of your world,"* he said. "I've spent all my life in prison. When I was a child I was an orphan and too ugly to be adopted. Now I am too beautiful to be let free.

**"How can you judge me, Amerika? after what you have done to me? Amerika, I am you. You are me. I am your image in the mirror! I am whatever you make me out to be!**

"I can take whatever they do to me. I like solitary confinement. I can take jail. When the pigs can no longer hurt you, they have no more power over you. You are then more powerful than they are."

After leaving Manson, Phil and I were visibly moved by his strength and personal magnetism. He was one of the most poetic and intense people we ever met, and he spoke from a world of experience we could not even imagine.

His words and courage inspired us and Phil and I felt great the rest of the day, overwhelmed by the depth of the experience of touching Manson's soul.

Manson's soul is easy to touch because it lays quite bare on the surface.

He said he was innocent of the Tate murders and was being persecuted by the pigs because of his lifestyle. About the only thing that angered us was his incredible male chauvinism.

Is Charlie innocent or guilty? What is innocence and what is guilt?

Can Amerika, after all it has done to Charlie Manson, now put him on trial? Whenever I think of Charlie Manson all I think is one fact:

**CHARLIE MANSON HAS SPENT 22 YEARS OF HIS LIFE BEHIND BARS.**

"Breathe some of that fresh air for me," a Black Muslim asked me as I was leaving Cook County Jail.

Watching TV news in jail is a trip.

Today we saw the riot of 30,000 kids who came to a city rock concert at Grant Park and ended up in a direct and unprovoked attack on the pigs, stoning pigs and burning police cars. Every time a pig fell in a pool of blood, pandemonium swept the jail tier with the blacks and whites applauding and cheering. "I hear ya! I hear ya!" Wally shouted.

As one big roly-poly pig fell over himself on the ground trying to catch a fleeing youth, the prisoners roared in laughter.

When the pigs caught and then clubbed and beat demonstrators, the prisoners shouted out, "POLICE BRUTALITY! POLICE BRUTALITY!"

Give your life to chance.
Let Serendipity become your guide.
History is made by accident.
**Be ready to discover what you were not looking for.**

Jail is a good place for meditation.
You are forced by the barrenness and asceticism of your environment deeper into yourself and you can recall with graphic detail feelings and experiences of days long past.
There are no distractions to occupy your mind.
The outside world does not exist. Your universe is now two walls, one steel door and a set of bars.
You feel like the animal in a zoo you saw as a kid. Your dreams, fantasies and memories are all you have. And the forced asceticism brings out your soul most clearly.
You remember minute details and feelings. Your thinking has a clarity to it.

Toleration or repression—both help us grow. The best is a cycle—a little bit of repression, then some toleration, then repression, then toleration. Too much repression or too much toleration are both bad for the growth of the revolution. After Nixon and Agnew we need some toleration!

I rarely meet a couple I dig as a couple.
Usually the dependency is so embarrassing that my eyes hurt. Or their special relationship excludes you, and you feel not part of their collective. With almost every couple I meet, I enjoy being with each of the partners *alone*.

Some stoned yippies lost their minds and fantasized an invasion of Disneyland of thousands, thousands, no millions! of freaks. They wanted it to happen—so they said it *was* happening.
Truth is stranger than fiction, but fiction creates truth.
They rushed to the telephone to make 300 long-distance telephone calls all over the country—free, thanks to Spiro Agnew's credit card. *Thank you, Spiro.*
They zapped every wall in California with spray paint announcing: "Yippies in Disneyland, August 6. See you there."
They sent announcements and posters showing Mickey Mouse with an AK 47 machine gun to every above- and underground paper in the country, and also to all the police chiefs in California.
The theme of the day was: Whatever happens happens. Don't ask: What's

going to happen at Disneyland? Make it happen!

The pigs decided to make *their* fantasy happen. They began riot control training in formation, with gas masks and machine guns.

The papers reported yippie announcements that 100,000 freaks were coming. Mayors, police officials held emergency meetings. Scared officials sought someone—anyone—to negotiate with. But there was no one.

The yippies were nowhere to be found.

Walt Disney could not have drawn a more joyous cartoon.

Hundreds of freaks rushed the gates and broke up into different gangs running through Disneyland stealing children from their parents, outrunning pigs and hanging the Viet Cong flag outside Frontier Fort and the New Nation flag over City Hall.

Freaks liberated Tom Sawyer's island, smoked dope in teepees in the Indian Village.

*Bernardine Dohrn and Jeff Jones drove straight people home with a massive marshmallow fight, then led a charge on the Bank of Amerika, breaking its window.*

And finally late in the afternoon all the yippie gangs got together in a victory march down the main street of Disneyland chanting: "Free Charlie Manson!"

The pigs attacked the yippies and ferocious fighting followed. The management closed Disneyland early for the second time in its history. The first time was the Kennedy Assassination.

The yippies rushed home in time to see themselves on Cronkite.

"Wow! Look at that line of pigs guarding Snow White's Castle!" The action—now as a myth—went around the world.

The yippies issued a statement: "Today we brought Amerika to its knees. We closed it down."

Disneyland officials announced that longhairs were forever banned from the park.

We joined Khrushchev, the first yippie to be banned from Fantasyland.

Some longhairs got pissed off at the yippies, saying, "You ruined it for all longhairs."

One yippie arrested for jumping the barbed wire fence pleaded not guilty by reason of insanity. A strike of employees began the next day at Disneyland.

It was the perfect yippie action: a stoned myth spreading by media and gossip, then followed by anarchy, pig overreaction, spontaneity, fun and fantastic theater, minor repression and a worldwide legend.

What happened that day in Disneyland? I don't know. I wasn't there.

I made all this up.

*You can make it up too because you were there like me, weren't you?*

I was invited to come to England to do the David Frost Show. I got a free

ticket to Europe from the English publishers of *Do It!* and I was on my way. At the same time the Youth International Party had just sent a delegation to Algeria to celebrate Tim and Rosemary Leary's arrival there.

Tim Leary's birthday and Bobby Seale's birthday fall on the same day, and a huge cake and party took place in Eldridge's home in Algiers with Eldridge, other Black Panther fugitives, Tim, Rosemary, yippies Jennifer Dohrn, Stew Albert, Brian Flanagan, Anita Hoffman, Martin Kenner, Jonah Raskin.

Leary, who escaped from the USA disguised as a straight, bald-headed businessman, got a lifetime subscription to LSD.

Rosemary is also a wanted fugitive with Tim, having skipped her probation.

Jennifer Dohrn had lived for two years in Watts organizing in a bra factory as a member of a small, ideological Marxist sect. She got turned on by revolutionary culture and the Weatherpeople and dropped out, and is now a yippie tripping around the country turning on freaks and building the nation with her soul.

While in Algeria she and Eldridge pulled a yippie trick by saying "Miss Dohrn" would be there, setting off international gossip among CIA agents that her Weather sister, Bernardine, was there.

A week was spent requesting the Algerian government to grant Tim and Rosemary asylum, which they did, and then Tim, Jennifer, Martin and Don Cox, one of the many Panther fugitives living with Eldridge, went off to ride camels in Egypt and visit Palestinian guerrilla camps.

Stew and Brian met Phil Ochs and me in France and we started our European adventure with the goals of turning children against parents, creating the Youth International Party everywhere, having an uproarious time—and then, if possible, to make the trip completely successful, getting deported.

We arrived in Amsterdam. It was like returning to one's homeland although we had never been there.

Yippie was born in Amsterdam, the child of Provo.

It was in Amsterdam where freaks first appeared to throw smoke bombs at the Queen, feed speed to the Queen's horses, hand out blank pieces of paper as leaflets, put white bicycles all over the city for free use and threaten to put LSD in the water.

Now the provos had become Kabouters and they escalated their zap tactics to include building a new nation.

The Kabouters are attempting to create a communal society within capitalist Holland.

They are creating their own economic and living base. The Kabouters have their own farms to grow food, factories, bookstores, restaurants, liberated houses.

They won five seats in the City Council and at the first meeting one of the Kabouters lit up a foot-long joint. This year bombs began bursting in Holland in the struggle between the Establishment and the youths.

Everyone smokes pot and hash everywhere—in public restaurants, clubs, on the streets. It isn't legal but the pigs don't bust. It felt so good, so liberating, to be able to smoke pot wherever you want to! You can even blow pot smoke in a pig's face and he won't bust you.

We stayed with Steve Davidson in one of the houses the Kabouters have seized from the city and are using for squatting. Steve is Minister of Offense of the Kabouters. His parents were both killed by the Nazis and Steve wears a mazuzah, a Jewish symbol, around his neck along with Arab beads.

*Hundreds of Amerikan underground papers were all over the floor, and the Jefferson Airplane and Creedence Clearwater Revival filled the room with sound.*

Kabouters and yippies began creating an international pact, "A Treaty of Civil War," threatening war on everyone from travel agents to advertising agents and other capitalist pigs.

We toasted the pact with a joint. The Kabouters promised that if Bernardine Dohrn is ever captured by the FBI, the Kabouters will retaliate against the Dutch government, "and make them pay for it."

**WE ARE EVERYWHERE.**

We arrived in England and as we moved through immigration an official opened a huge book and looked for our names. They were there.

"Please sit down and make yourself comfortable, we have some checking to do with the Home Office," he said.

The English pigs are so polite. They kill you with politeness. The man came back.

"I'm sorry, gentlemen, the man we have to talk with is on the tube on his way home and we're waiting for him to arrive. You came at a bad hour, you see. Please be patient."

Two hours later as we were eating fish and chips the guard came back and said, "The Home Office has granted you a one-week visa to stay in our country. Hope you enjoy it." Stew and I winked.

"They'll be sorry they let us in," Stew said quietly.

We had a wild group. Besides Stew and myself, there was Phil Ochs, who sang at all our European rallies and opened and closed press conferences in France and Amsterdam with music. Phil brought tears to our eyes one night in France when we all sat stoned in someone's apartment after a huge French meal and he sang.

Phil's songs are our generation's history set to poetry and music and he's always on the front lines of all the battles from the Pentagon to Chicago with his guitar.

Then there was Brian Flanagan. It was far out introducing Brian to the French at rallies! He's a Weatherman and last October he ran through the streets of Chicago in the "Days of Rage" with lead pipes attacking pigs. Brian was accused of breaking the neck of the city's top prosecution lawyer, Richard Elrod, as Elrod tried to tackle him in the streets.

Elrod lay in a hospital paralyzed for months. At his trial Brian cut his hair, put on a suit and tie, said he was a carpenter, said Elrod broke his neck when he hit a wall in a flying tackle and that he had come to Chicago to a "peace rally." Then he smiled and charmed the jury.

The verdict: not guilty!

Brian ran outside the courtroom to hold a press conference, ripping off his suit and tie and saying he was going right back into the streets! A few weeks later Brian became a yippie and pulled the yippiest trick.

He announced that he was running for sheriff against Elrod! He got 67 votes but he probably won 'cause, as we know, all Chicago elections are fixed.

The David Frost Show would be live.

Far out!

Dynamite!

Live TV is dead in Amerika.

Everything is pre-packaged, censored, refined, catalogued, then fed to the public. That way, no mistakes can be made. No surprises, nothing unplanned.

No reality!

So, true to our nature as yippies, we set out to destroy live TV in England! Spread a little cheer and repression wherever we go . . .

Yippies, White Panthers, underground newspaper writers, video freaks and other free spirits crowded into a dope-filled room conspiring to take over the Frost Show. We'd get as many tickets as we could from various respectable sources like media and book publishers and fill the studio audience with freaks.

We decided that a few of us would talk for a bit to get some ideas across to the viewers but we all agreed that taking over the show would be a much deeper and more revolutionary message than any dialogue we could have with David Frost.

Instead of the celebrity guests representing the movement as individual spokesmen, all the yippies would take over the show. The energy in the room was fantastic!

Everyone was coming up with ideas and taking on responsibility for carrying them out.

Everyone was talking at once!

"I'll bring the dope!"

"I'll get orange smoke bombs!"

"I'll bring crepe paper and water pistols!"

We broke up into smaller groups to do work and planned to meet half an hour before the show.

"It'll be a party! We'll have a party on TV! Let people see what our bloody culture is all about anyway," said Mick Farren of the White Panthers.

Frost sent over three taxis to pick us up. He was planning his own funeral live on national TV and he didn't even know it.

Yippies dressed in suits and dresses filled the studio audience, then took off their hats and clothes and the studio audience became a costume ball.

Frost suspected something because he was as white as a ghost. For 15 minutes we psychologically pistol-whipped Frost, exposing his racism and snobbery, calling him a "plastic man." Then someone pulled out a joint and began smoking it. Frost squirmed nervously. He tried to ignore it but I offered him a puff.

"No, thanks," he said, hoping it would go away.

The pulling out of the joint was the signal for the stampede. Yippies began pouring out of the studio audience and onto the stage, the little platform where Frost sits with his guests.

Frost began to panic—the hordes were invading.

And it was all happening live! Seventy million English women and men were glued to their tellies, living in a true global village. Watching the David Frost Show in England on Saturday night was as common as tea with milk. The producers could do nothing about it but let the chaos continue.

As the yippies took the stage surrounding Frost, one male yippie embraced David, kissed him on the cheek and said, "Greetings from Gay Lib, David."

Some yippies began taking off their clothes. Yippies ran down racism and sexism in angry street talk. "Fuck" zoomed over the airwaves. The liberation

of energy on the show was astounding! Nobody was paying any attention to Frost.

Someone yelled, "David Frost is dead! It's our show now!" Frost freaked out.

He leaped out of his seat and ran into the studio audience, surrendering his show to the yippies.

I don't know if we made the best use out of the free time. Everything was happening so fast at the same time. Commotion, commotion, everything was commotion. The takeover was communication itself.

Frost turned to Robert Ardrey, an author who has this theory that humans are no different than the ape. Ardrey said, "You see, it just proves it—they're infantile animals up there."

Frost tried to recapture his show by asking me a question from the studio audience. By this time he was shaking.

With Frost's mouth wide open a yippie fired a water pistol right at his face, splashing water all over him on live TV.

That water action by an English yippie liberated the rest of us. As Stew put it, "Before that happened I would have shot a pig in the back before I'd squirt him in the face with a water pistol. Squirting him in the face just seemed so degrading to the pig. I don't like to embarrass people. I was shocked, but then I was liberated when I saw it happen. I feel now I can do it—I'm a real yippie."

Frost finally saved Western civilization by switching to a commercial. He then moved the show into another studio.

Paddywagons and pigs surrounded the studio.

The pigs came up to me and said, "Pardon me, sir, could you please tell me if you are Mr. Rubin?" I said no, and ran into the streets as fast as I could. All of us began running, with the English dope and vice squad in hot pursuit. We outran them and got away.

## GREAT BRITAIN FREAKED OUT!

Members of Parliament began demanding an independent inquiry into live television. All the papers sensationally blazed page-one headlines: "Yippies Invade Frost!"

Some editorials suggested that the whole thing may have been a put-on staged by the yippies and Frost to boost his ratings. The bourgeois press was very upset that we got paid $400 to go on the show.

But everywhere we went in the streets English people, working people, stopped to congratulate us. We were recognized everywhere we went and people dug it.

"Did you have fun watching it?" we asked.

"Sure did!" was everyone's response.

Everyone had 1,000 questions to ask. It was on everyone's lips. It was the most successful pure media event I'd ever seen and it showed that through TV one event can really sock it to a nation.

England had become a village.

There was hardly any place you could go where people weren't talking about it, recognizing us and taking sides.

TV had become real to peoples' lives.

The English hippies, street people and freaks got very high off an action they created and made happen.

They formed the British Youth International Party and began planning seizures of newspapers and churches. Freaks felt a lot of energy in the streets and began getting together.

Newspapers ran front-page editorials demanding an end to the yippie invasion of Britain.

Parliament debated our fate.

Finally Regis McCauley, the Home Secretary, called a big press conference to order the Amerikan yippies out of England in 24 hours. We issued a counterstatement telling McCauley to "**GO TO HELL!**"

The pressure was great and we needed spiritual guidance. We decided to go visit Karl Marx's grave. It took rides in three English double-decker buses to get there. We found ourselves standing before a giant true-to-life bust of Karl with the words: "Workers of All Lands—Unite—The philosophers have only interpreted the world in various ways. The point however is to change it." Karl was saying: Do It!

We lit up a few joints and got high with Karl. I put my head near the tomb to see if he'd speak to us. I apologized to him for all the nasty things I said about him in my yippie anti-ideology days, things like "Karl Marx never watched television." We finally had to leave because the cemetery closed.

We wanted to leave something permanent with Karl.

We dug a hole in the ground near his grave.

I buried a White Panther button deep in the soil, forever resting in the earth with Karl Marx. *If you go out there in 10 years, you'll find it there.*

We had a 2 o'clock appointment to see Bernadette Devlin at the House of Commons, where she is a member. It had been arranged by a friend at *Oz*, the underground magazine.

We were sitting in the big waiting room overwhelmed by the incredible palace the bourgeoisie had built for itself when in bounced Bernadette smiling, a bit embarrassed at the place, almost suppressing a giggle—sort of like, "What are all us freaks doing in here?"—then winking to us and saying, "Want to have a drink in here?"

*It was real yippie for Bernadette to invite us into her world. Her boozing with us would fill her fellow MPs' mouths with shocked gossip.*

She led us through hallway after hallway, then door after door, past pigs, members of the House, foreign dignitaries and into the Inner Sanctum, a little pub where only Members of Parliament and their guests can drink.

Here we were, drinking ale inside the luxury of Parliament with Bernadette

Devlin while in another part of the same building Members of Parliament passed a motion demanding that the Home Secretary eject us from the country!

Bernadette had seen the Frost Show and dug it. She began telling us the situation in Ireland and how she didn't raise much money in the USA when Irish nationalists discovered that she was a socialist and anti-imperialist. "They didn't like me supporting the Black Panthers," she said.

She stressed that what is going on in Ireland is a class war, not a religious war.

"The British want to make it seem like a conflict between Catholics and Protestants," she said, "but both the Catholic and Protestant working class is exploited."

Bernadette kept nodding her head and smiling. She was having fun. "I'm here in Parliament to give them a rough time and I'm doing it," Bernadette said. "We can't win anything in this place."

We told Bernadette that the American revolutionary movement supported the Irish struggle for freedom from British control and for socialism. Bernadette had spent the summer in jail for inciting to riot and had come out a few weeks earlier to take her elected seat in Parliament.

We talked for two hours, then Bernadette's question was coming up on the House floor. "Once a week the Prime Minister comes and you get to publicly ask him a question, that is, if they ever get to me." We exchanged addresses, embraced and said we'd see her in Ireland.

The Home Secretary ordered us out of Great Britain but we came up with a killer idea. We had a day to get out of England but we decided not to leave.

We'd go underground.

We'd go to Belfast.

The Irish do not consider Belfast part of Great Britain. The British, meanwhile, militarily occupy and colonize Belfast. We'd say we had left England and had entered Ireland and it would expose the unpopular Vietnam-like occupation of Ireland by Britain.

It was great politics and the Frost takeover had given us the media exposure to make the point.

We disguised ourselves as nuns and priests and snuck into Belfast.

We made contact with several revolutionary groups and finally met the yippies and anarchists of Ireland, who disguised us and drove us around Belfast showing us the incredible abject poverty of the workers in Belfast.

Walking the streets were British soldiers, in single file so they wouldn't get caught together in sniper fire, carrying machine guns with fully loaded clips.

It was the first time I had even been in a city of guerrilla war.

We arranged secretly to meet in a pub with a photographer to take a smiling picture of Stew and me drinking large glasses of Guinness Stout, to win the hearts and throats of the Irish working class.

We held out for two days while the Irish puppet police under orders from

the British were searching for us. Finally, we decided to turn ourselves in. We called a press conference and after it a gang of plainclothes Irish police grabbed us and stuffed us into cars as we shouted: **"ENGLAND HAS NO AUTHORITY HERE! WE'RE IN IRELAND, NOT ENGLAND!"**

We were taken to a British jail and for an hour the narcotics pigs searched our clothes, suitcases, and bodies for dope. It was the most thorough dope search any of us ever had.

We were then served fish and chips and tea, and we went to bed.

In the morning our jail guards went outside and brought us all the newspapers and we were served breakfast in bed.

We were just speculating what was going to happen to us when our jail door opened and 15 pigs barged in and ordered Stew and me to pack up and get our belongings. They put us into a paddywagon and drove us to the airport where they escorted us up the ramp of the airplane, put us on the plane and watched us take off in a jetliner heading straight for New York.

A bloodless, cold deportation.

We had violated no English law, but we were deported as "undesirable aliens." National boundaries are a joke.

Passports are bullshit.

The free woman and free man should be able to go anywhere.

No state should be able to tell us where we can travel.
We yippies resolve to destroy all nations and national boundaries.

*Getting deported is a trip. You go home in style. And the price is right.*
*It's free.*
*The deporting government pays for it.*
*Do it some time.*

For years I fucked around with my body.

I didn't exercise enough, I drank too many Cokes, I even used to pop ritalin, a psychic energizer, for speeches and things. I had coffee with white sugar and a donut for breakfast and ate my big meal at supper.

Enough of that shit! The best speed is natural body energy and since I've been on a health trip I've been in great physical and psychological shape, living each day intensely and deeply.

**The revolutionary culture should free itself from the suicide trip most Amerikans are on.** It is a counterrevolutionary act to smoke cigarettes. I cannot believe anyone is a revolutionary if he or she smokes. We should create a spirit in our culture which discourages smokers from smoking.

The result will be Pig Amerika smokes cigarettes; revolutionary America does not.

Yippies now eat our big meals at breakfast, including meat, to get energy for the day. Makes a lot of sense, doesn't it? Big meals at dinner just mean bloated, full stomachs, falling off to sleep and dying.

It's also a bullshit lifestyle based around the phony eight-hour day.

A good thing to remember is: *Eat breakfast like a queen or king, lunch like a princess or prince, supper like a pauper.*

We should also wash Coke out of our system. Coke is the essence of Imperialism, a poison drink. Coka-colonialism.

We yippies should organize a campaign in the youth culture against cigarettes and Coke and encourage people to enjoy a real hedonistic life. Yippies are now into natural foods, honey instead of white sugar, plenty of vitamin C, lots of vitamins, orange juice.

Some yippies also do a half hour **isometric** exercises a day with the Tinsolator or Bullworker and we smoke pot as soon as we wake up and we stay stoned all day.

We have to build a guerrilla army so we all gotta be strong. To really dig life a healthy body is key. Why commit suicide when living is so much fun?

Yippies rip off vitamins and health foods from the profit-gouging stores. I hope you stole this book. A stolen book is much more fun to read. You feel so high after stealing it!

**DON'T LOOK BACK.**

They are trying to rip off our culture. They are smoking our dope, wearing our clothes and talking like us. They are selling us our culture. They are trying to take the revolutionary sting out of our culture by making it a *style*. They refuse to admit the truth: that our culture is an affirmation of Life, and the negation of the Death Culture.

We cannot be bought off. We want too much. We do not seek civil liberties for freaks—we want a revolution freeing everyone. We do not want longhair capitalists or longhair policemen or women. A capitalist is a capitalist is a pig is a pig, no matter how long the hair.

*We do not want a longhair Mayor Stokes.*

As long as the Death Culture exists, the Life Culture cannot be secure. We will build our culture and destroy capitalist, Christian culture. We are not afraid to die or kill 'cause we love life so much.

Only when you no longer fear death can you really dig life.

**WE LIVE EVERY MOMENT AS IF IT'S OUR LAST.**

Re-reading this book I realize all the things I forgot to put in.

I forgot to say that Julius Hoffman inherited from his wife a factory which makes bowling balls and war materials for Vietnam. Our judge, a war profiteer!

I forgot to say that after our escapade in England the Board of Directors of Penguin Books met and voted not to publish *Do It!* after signing a contract for the book five months earlier. The noose of repression tightens.

I forgot to say that we ran into Eugene McCarthy in the streets in George-town in Washington, D.C., the other day. He was friendly. He didn't bait us as revolutionaries, although we baited his liberalism. We asked him why he didn't speak out against the repression of the Black Panthers. "Half the people in jail in Amerika don't belong there," he said. We asked him if there were going to be concentration camps in Amerika soon. **"YES," HE SAID, "AND THEY'LL SAY THEY ARE DOING IT FOR 'HUMANE REASONS.' "**

I forgot to say a lot. This book ends where it began. I gotta learn to live with imperfection. I hope you're stoned and I hope this book set off energy in your head and body.

**One of the great adventures in life is for you and me to discover what we really think. We hear so many voices in our own heads; it's often hard to hear our own.**

I did *not* forget to say: *I love you.*

Jerry

# PHOTOGRAPHY

LAYOUT/DESIGN: Nguyen Ai Quoc Intercommunal Shitworkers Local 110
super/vision: dawg!


Typeset at O.B.U. Typesetters, Inc., ONE BIG UNION!
Don't mourn. ORGANIZE! — Joe Hill